The British Natural History Collection

Volume 8

PINE MARTENS

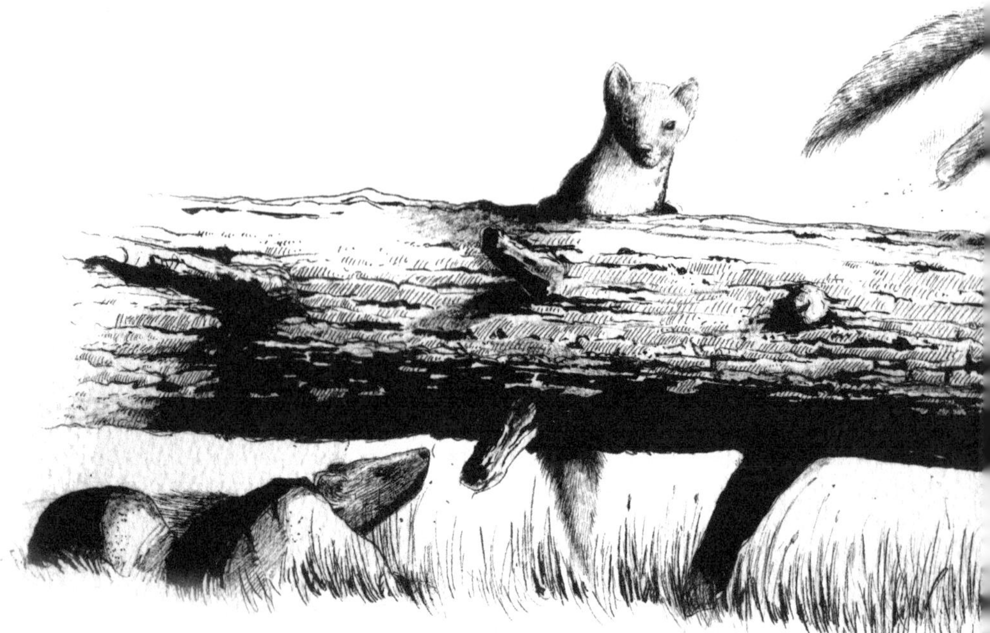

PINE MARTENS

Johnny Birks

Illustrations by Antony Griffiths
Photographs by Terry Whittaker

Whittet Books

Whittet Books Ltd
1 St John's Lane
Stansted
Essex CM24 8JU
mail@whittetbooks.com
www.whittetbooks.com

First published 2017
Reprinted 2020 (with updates)

Text © Johnny Birks 2017, 2020
Illustrations and *Pine Marten* painting © Antony Griffiths 2017
Photographs © Terry Whittaker

This publication is in copyright. Subject to statutory exception and to the provisions of relevant collective licensing agreements, no part of this publication may be reproduced, transmitted or stored in a retrieval system, in any form or by any means, without the prior permission of Whittet Books Ltd.

Whittet Books Ltd has no responsibility for the persistence or accuracy of URLs for external or third party internet websites referred to in this publication and does not guarantee that any content on such websites is, or will remain, accurate or appropriate.

A catalogue record for this publication is available from the British Library.

ISBN 978 1 873580 32 5

Designed by Lodge Graphics

CONTENTS

Acknowledgements	1
Preface	3
Marterns, martins, marts and martens	6
Martens in heraldry, legend, mythology and popular culture	10
Origins and close relatives	15
The Weasel Family	15
Early origins and evolutionary history	15
The *Martes* Complex	16
Stone Marten	20
Sable	25
Yellow-throated marten	26
Nilgiri marten	27
Japanese marten	28
American marten	28
Pacific marten	29
Pine marten history, genetics and distribution in Europe	29
Is the stone/beech marten native to the British Isles?	32
The body beautiful	36
Shape and movement	36
Coping with the cold	37
Body size and sexual dimorphism	38
Arboreal adaptations	40
Skull and teeth	44
Fur colour and moult	46
Horrendous history	49
Downhill from a Mesolithic heyday	49
The confusing pattern of the pine marten's decline in Britain and Ireland	49
Pine martens killed as vermin	50
Trapping for fur	51
Hunting with hounds	52
Game shooting	54
Habitat loss	55
Differences between Britain and Ireland	56
Where did martens survive and why?	57
Survival and slow, partial recovery	59
The 'mythical' martens of England and Wales	61
Current distribution and status	64
Ireland	64
Scotland	65
Wales	65
England	66
Modern marten habitats	67
Woodland specialist or habitat generalist?	67
Going underground in Nietoperek, Poland	71
Activity Patterns	73
'Gimme Shelter' – Dens and resting sites	74
Seeking elevation and insulation	74
Missing cavities	75
Where do pine martens sleep and breed?	76
Designing bedrooms and nurseries for martens	78
Field signs	80
The Joy of Scats	83
Heaven-scent!	83
Variations in form, texture and colour	84
The hip-wiggle (please don't try this at home!)	86
Scats for surveys	88
Scat detection dogs	91
The work of the Gene-genies	93
The pine marten's year	95
Social life and home range behaviour	97
Territoriality	97
Home range sizes	97
Social martens	100
Martelism	100
Foraging and food	102
A multi-skilled omnivore	102
The pine martens of Białowieża Forest	103
The predator-prey arms race	105
Continental variations in feeding ecology	106
Rodents rule	109

Pine marten diets in Britain and Ireland	110	predator	146
Why do Scottish pine martens prefer field voles?	111	How do pine martens and stone martens coexist?	146
Caching of food	115	Capercaillie capers	150
Marten communications	**116**	Grey squirrel control?	154
Scented messages	116	**Interactions with people**	**158**
Vocalisations	119	The teething pains of pine marten recovery	158
Tail-swishing	120	Mischievous media manipulation	158
Mating and breeding	**122**	The good, the bad and the delightfully cheeky	159
Breeding slow but long	122	Adapting to life with pine martens	161
The mating season	123	Protecting bird boxes	162
Delayed implantation and gestation	124	Roof martens	164
Birth dates and litter sizes	125	Protecting poultry and game	166
Mast and mice control the martens	125	Sustainable egg-collection?	168
Development of kits	126	Illegal trapping and killing of pine martens	169
Natal den relocation	128	Moving pine martens	171
Juvenile dispersal	129	Feeding and watching pine martens	172
The male 'teenage' phase	130	An evening with Pat and James's martens	176
Longevity	131	**Reintroductions and translocations**	**178**
How many martens?	**132**	Covert releases	178
Improving abundance estimates	132	The VWT's Pine Marten Recovery Project	179
National population estimates	133	**Studying pine martens**	**182**
The martens of Portlaw Woods, Eire	135	**Pine martens and the law**	**184**
The martens of Galloway Forest, Scotland	135	**Pine martens and commercial forestry**	**186**
Health and Safety	**137**	**Further reading**	**188**
Causes of mortality	137	**Sources of information and advice**	**189**
Street-fighting martens?	138	**Index**	**190**
Parasites and diseases	138		
Interactions with other wildlife	**144**		
Relations with foxes	144		
Adjusting to the return of a native			

The photographs are between pages 66 and 67.

ACKNOWLEDGEMENTS

For some reason that I have yet to fathom, the community of pine marten enthusiasts contains more than its fair share of delightfully bonkers people (yes, it takes one to know one). I am fortunate to have rubbed shoulders with many of them over the past 25 years; they have helped me to appreciate the pine marten's special charm; and their efforts and influence have helped to shape this book. They are far too many to name here, but I am grateful to them all. The main culprits are mentioned in the text, and a few more receive special mention below.

My time working for The Vincent Wildlife Trust between 1993 and 2007 was a precious opportunity to work on pine martens with some special people then and since. Thank you dear VWT chums, and to all volunteers who have supported the VWT's work on pine martens. I am also grateful to my colleagues in Swift Ecology who have tolerated my mustelid madness over the years.

A few people have been extra helpful: Lizzie Croose ensured I never missed any crucial marten news or publications; Jenny Macpherson, Hans Kleef, Tim Hofmeester, Laura Kubasiewicz and Josh Twining allowed access to valuable pre-publication data; Ian Francis, Colin Leslie, Kenny Kortland, Rob Coope, Allan Bantick and Matt Wilson helped me to understand bizarre reactions to the pine marten's recovery in Scotland, where *Pine Marten Diaries* were revelatory. I am grateful to Paddy Sleeman, Catherine O'Reilly, Pete Turner, Kate McAney, Declan O'Mahony, Emma Sheehy and David Tosh for Irish wisdom; in Wales Huw Denman and Tony Braithwaite were tireless allies in 'the quest'; I thank Henri Wijsman and Hans Kleef of the Werkgroep Boommarter Nederland for sharing their knowledge of Dutch pine martens; also thanks to Claire Poirson for French marten news and to Martin Noble for helpful insights; and to Andrzej Zalewski for showing me the magic of Białowieża Forest, where he studied pine martens in a near-pristine environment. Many of these people are members of the international Martes Working Group, which has inspired, informed and entertained me over the years.

I have been very lucky to work closely with two of the most devious minds I have ever encountered: John Messenger and John Martin have taught me that any problem can be solved through lateral thinking and use of the correct screwdriver. Our work on pine martens in Galloway Forest – greatly assisted by Shirley Martin – has been made possible by Forest Enterprise Scotland (FES) and the People's Trust for Endangered Species, and I am grateful to Geoff Shaw, Andrew Jarrott, Martin Webber and Gareth Ventress of FES for their support.

Hilary Macmillan, John Martin and Lizzie Croose kindly reviewed an early draft of this book. I thank Shirley Greenall for her guidance, and I salute Whittet Books for fostering the blend of science and humour that sets this series apart from the rest.

Finally, I am grateful to Helen for patiently enduring all those bouts of PMT (pine marten tension) and the frequent embarrassment of being married to an obsessive scat-sniffer. This book is dedicated to our amazing daughters, Lisa and Stacey.

PREFACE

I fell under the pine martens' spell a long time ago and have been fascinated by them ever since. I learnt early on that Professor Hale's heartfelt words – in his case inspired by a love of redshanks – applied equally to me: thus 'Life is too short not to spend it studying pine martens' has been my motto for years. Having been lucky enough to follow that dream and get to know such a charming animal, I happily echo the words of wildlife photographer James Moore: 'If there's a more bonny beast than the pine marten I've never seen it'.

As a keen young mammalogist, I was beguiled by the work of the Devon naturalist and photographer H. G. Hurrell. I treasured his early publications on pine martens: notably the glossy 1963 monograph in the *Sunday Times* series illustrated with photographs of Hurrell's captive but sometimes free-range martens and enriched by descriptions of how he trained them to leap from tree to tree with his pole-mounted *martinet* device; and in 1980 *Fling, the Story of the Pine Marten* which, although a fictional story, was based on Hurrell's unsurpassed knowledge at the time, from having kept and bred pine martens for thirty years.

Later, my quests for information via early internet searches in the late 1980s – guided by family friend Doug Doughty – were as hilarious as they were hapless: I learnt about *Doc Martens*, 'a range of iconic shoes with air-conditioned soles, famed for their rebellious self-expression'; then, smugly entering the marten's Latin name – *Martes* – I discovered how many important events had occurred on Tuesdays in the Spanish-speaking world. Thankfully, information is more accessible now, albeit mainly in scientific papers and survey reports, with Paddy Sleeman's 1989 Whittet book *Stoats and Weasels, Polecats and Martens* a popular exception.

This new book focuses upon what we know about pine martens in Britain and Ireland on the far western edge of their distribution, where recent research has advanced our knowledge in leaps and bounds. But given our extreme location – pine marten-wise – we should appreciate that our wet, windswept and deforested islands offer atypical conditions for martens compared with the rest of their huge Eurasian range. So, where necessary, I have drawn on continental studies to reflect the full range of marten behaviour.

As with *Polecats*, the marten's story is ultimately a positive one: of a carnivore pushed close to extinction in Britain a hundred years ago (and rather later in Ireland) and then grudgingly allowed to recover. As part of that recovery, thrillingly, pine martens have recently been translocated from Scotland to boost struggling populations in Wales; and where martens are tolerated in their strongholds, their mischievous interactions with people are on the increase. As Matt Wilson wryly told me, based on his experiences in the Scottish Highlands, 'wherever there's a marten, there's a story!' How I have enjoyed telling some of those stories in this book.

Beyond its cheeky charm, for me there is a powerful symbolism about the pine marten: it is a resurgent survivor of our ancestors' abuse of predators; and its association with woodland and old, characterful trees means that it cradles the ancient spirit of the wildwood in its furry paws. Its recovery is a tiny but vital counter-current to the horrific biodiversity loss that defines the 'Anthropocene', evidence that it is not all one-way traffic, that we still have reasons to be hopeful and continue striving to conserve our wildlife.

The pine marten is the brightest yet most fragile star in our mustelid firmament: fragile because there are some who resent its recovery and the challenges it presents; and the slow-breeding pine marten struggles where populations are culled. This book explores the conflicts – real and perceived – that now test the tolerance of those who live with pine martens once more. It reveals a painful gulf between those willing to seek sustainable and legal solutions to the inevitable challenges, and those who persist in tackling threats to poultry and game in old-fashioned ways. Furthermore, an influential minority clings to the Victorian dogma that carnivores and birds of prey are bad for our wildlife, despite the wealth of evidence that predators and predation are essential components of healthy ecosystems.

We need to help them see the light, and I hope this book will play its part.

Finally, I had considered apologising for the shockingly extensive text devoted to scats (as marten poo is called), but that would have been dishonest: scats are crucial to marten enthusiasts; they are our meat and drink, figuratively speaking; so, it is only right that I try to explain why, at some length.

MARTERNS, MARTINS, MARTS AND MARTENS

As with so many other animals, the pine marten's English name has evolved over time, and this may have involved human confusion with similar species along the way. Writing between 1656 and 1691 John Aubrey pronounced *'Upon the disafforestations, the marterns were utterly destroyed in North Wilt'*; in 1768 Pennant wrote of *martins*, as did Goldsmith in 1840; and this name persisted until it was replaced with *martens* in the late 1800s, reportedly to avoid confusion among naturalists with birds of the same name. Sometimes, in old English, the name *marten cat* was used, and marten was often abbreviated to *mart*; and in old English this abbreviation sometimes carried the prefix sweet or clean, as in *sweet-mart* or *clean mart* to distinguish the pine marten from its more strongly scented relative the polecat or *foulmart*. Other variations in old English include *martron, martlett, merteron* and even *matron*. In addition to these mart-related names, the pine marten was known by more descriptive local names, such as *tree-cat* and *cat-squirrel*, as in the old Cleveland saying 'A cat squirrel could gae fra Commondil ti Glaisdil thruff treeas an nut put fooit t't grund, yan-tahm' (this refers to the extensive former forest of that part of north-east England, with the distance described being about eight miles).

A more recent and curiously descriptive local English name for pine martens is *club tails*: in his 1970 book *The Fenland Molecatcher*, Arthur Randall writes 'Martens, or *club tails* as we call them in these parts, are occasionally found near Waldersea [near Wisbech in Cambridgeshire]. Over the past five or six years three have been killed here – I shot the third in February 1969 and left its body lying in the snow which had fallen overnight. I wished, afterwards, that I had taken it home because so many people had never seen one'. And Colin Simms uses the term *clubtails* in his poem *Marten and Wild Cat* published by Shearsman Books in 2004. However, in *A Natural History of British and Foreign Quadrupeds* (published in 1843) James Fennell tells us that *clubtail* was then a Yorkshire name for the stoat.

As for the other languages of Britain and Ireland, the names previously or currently in use for the pine marten are *bele* (Welsh), *taghan* (Scottish Gaelic), *cat crainn* (Irish Gaelic) and *mertrick* (Scottish dialect). Some of these have taken root as place names to remind us how pine martens were prominent in our ancestors' consciousness. For example, in Wales the landscape is peppered with features containing the word *bele* or variations thereon: so in Ceredigion there is a *Nant Bele* (Marten Stream), in Carmarthenshire there is an *Afon Bele* (Marten River), in Snowdonia there is a *Castell y Bele* (Marten's Castle) and across Wales martens are similarly linked to features such as *bryn* (hill), *cwrt* (court), *cors* or *gors* (marsh or swamp), *ffynnon* (spring, well or fountain) and *plas* (mansion); finally, a rocky outcrop high up in Cadair Idris in southern Snowdonia is called *Tap y Bele* because there, according to local knowledge (with thanks to Rhys Gwyn), a pine marten once bit a lady climber on the bottom.

Considering that the Celtic precursors of modern Welsh were spoken across much of Britain up until the medieval period, my Welsh language guru Huw Denman suggests we should not be surprised if *bele* was also used to name features beyond the Welsh border, especially in those areas of northern England and southern Scotland that retained Cumbric as a language into the medieval period; and the same goes for Brythonic in the west and south-west of England. So, might Bells Crags and Catbells in Cumbria be marten-related rather than campanological? Equally, it is tempting to view the various rocky sites in the Cumbrian Lake District named *Mart Crag* (one near Coniston, one near the Langdale Pikes – below *Martcrag Moor* – and another on Lingmoor Fell, with a *Mart Fold* nearby) as linked to the northern English abbreviation for marten (though *mart* is also a northern English abbreviation of market).

As part of his eighteenth-century binomial system, Linnaeus used a double dose of the Latin word for marten to create the pine marten's scientific name *Martes martes*, thereafter leaving the Spanish-speakers to wonder why he chose to name such an attractive animal *Tuesday tuesday*. Today several western European languages have a similar word for marten, suggesting a common Latin origin: so, we have *Marten* in English and Norwegian; *Martre* in French; *Marder* in German; *Marter* in Dutch; *Marta* in Portuguese and Spanish; and *Martora* in Italian.

As we shall explore further, early naturalists and zoologists recognised two types of marten occurring widely in Europe – now known as the pine marten and the stone or beech marten – and the nomenclature became messier as names were amended to separate them as shown in the table below. In some early English texts, the animals were separated on the basis of differences in the colour of their throat and chest, but most names reflected the pine marten's stronger association with trees and the stone marten's preference for rocky or craggy places. As a consequence, the original marten name later carried a prefix or suffix relating to woods, trees, crags and stones.

Language	Martes martes	Martes foina
English	Yellow-breasted marten	White-breasted marten
English	Pine-Martin	Common martin
English	Pine-weasel	Martin
English	Pine marten	Beech marten, Stone marten, House marten
Welsh	*Belagoed* ('wood marten')	*Bela Graig* ('crag marten')
German	*Baummarder* ('tree marten')	*Steinmarder* ('stone marten')
French	*Martre des Pins* ('marten of pines')	*Fouine*
Dutch	*Boommarter* ('tree marten')	*Steenmarter* ('stone marten')

Although the arboreal links are misleading if some specific ecological dependence is assumed, there is a geographical logic to the 'pine' and 'beech' prefixes added by early naturalists to separate the two European martens. For the pine marten is a cold-adapted inhabitant of the northern conifer-dominated forests; while the stone or beech marten has a more southerly distribution in which broad-leaved trees such as beech are dominant (an earlier Latin specific name for the stone or beech marten was *fagorum*, which refers to the beech tree). Of course, pine martens live happily in many woodlands where pines and other coniferous trees are scare or absent; and equally many stone or beech martens now live in towns and cities without a beech tree in sight.

The collective noun for a group of pine martens – if such a thing ever occurs in a rather solitary species – is a *richesse*. This is a medieval word, the modern equivalent of which is 'richness', which is probably linked to the quality and value of the pine marten's fur. This fur-based appreciation is a recurring theme in historical references to martens as we shall see later.

MARTENS IN HERALDRY, LEGEND, MYTHOLOGY AND POPULAR CULTURE

Originally valued mainly as fur-bearers, with their pelts commanding higher prices than those of most other mammals, martens have featured in European culture over many centuries. In Croatia (where today martens are acknowledged by rural communities as controllers of rodents) marten pelts were used as units of value by medieval traders, so today the Croatian currency is the *Kuna*, which is also the Croatian word for pine marten, and each coin bears an image of the animal. Perhaps for similar reasons pine martens appear on flags, coats of arms and other insignia in various countries in Central Europe. For example, in the eastern part of the Czech Republic, in Vsetín District, lies the small village of Kunovice (population 653). The official flag and municipal coat of arms of the village portrays a pair of erect pine martens supporting what appears to be an ironing board. The village must have taken its name partly from the Czech word for marten – *Kuna;* and, unless I have misinterpreted the imagery, the rest of the name could be something to do with ironing…?

Closer to home, there is a heraldic reference to pine martens in the journal *Private Eye* (*Eye* 1443), in which a correspondent writes, 'I now also have a faux Scottish passport issued by 'Auld Scotica' with the depiction on the front cover of the Loch Ness Monster and Pine Martin (*sic*) rampant with bagpipes passant'.

As with so many wild animals – and especially the predatory ones – myths about pine martens have been enshrined as fact or folklore by our more gullible ancestors. The most bizarre is the belief that the tip of the pine marten's fluffy tail concealed a claw or nail with which it could cause great harm to other living things, and some non-living too.

Martens have an important role in Native American culture and mythology, featuring as clan animals in some tribes. In the Great Lakes region of North America and Canada the Ojibwe Indians have seven clans, one of which is the *Waabizheshi Odoodeman* or Marten Clan. Through the Martes Working Group I met Jonathan Gilbert of the Great Lakes Indian Fish and Wildlife Commission, who studies the cultural importance and relationship between Waabizeshi (the American pine marten) and the Ojibwe Indians: the links are utilitarian as well as ceremonial; and clan members draw spiritual strength and guidance from wild martens as suggested by the following text:

'The small agile marten is limber, quick tempered, ferocious, has quick reflexes and is an excellent hunter. Members of the Marten Clan carry these characteristics and as a result are the strategists, warriors and builders within their community.'

Inspired by Jonathan's work on the links between American Indian culture and marten ecology, a senior member of The Vincent Wildlife Trust now has a magnificent totemic image of a Waabizeshi tattooed on her left calf.

Beyond their role as clan animals, martens feature frequently in the mythology of other American Indian tribes. Unlike the weasel and wolverine, which are usually the bad guys, martens are generally portrayed in a positive light as lucky spirits, brave heroes and skilled, determined hunters. The marten has special meaning to the Mi'kmaq tribe as the first animal to sacrifice itself as food for the human race. The elders and artists of the Kootenai tribe from the Flathead Indian Reservation in western Montana compiled *How Marten got his spots: and other Kootenai Indian stories*; this book was originally

Tattoo of a Waabizeshi (American pine marten), with special thanks to Jenny Macpherson for intimate access.

intended to educate younger members of the tribe about their history and culture; in the title story apparently Marten learns a hard lesson about obedience!

Pine martens have inspired poets, ancient and modern, from the composer of an early Welsh lullaby to the current naturalist-poet Colin Simms. In the late sixth century the bard Aneurin wrote the lullaby Pais Dinogad (Dinogad's Smock) about a hunter and the impressive list of animals he kills while wearing his marten-skin smock, the first two lines of which are (in modern Welsh spelling):

Pais Dinogad fraith fraith,
O grwyn balaod ban wraith.

Which roughly translates (with thanks to Huw Denman) as:

Dinogad's smock is speckled speckled,
from the skins of martens it was made.

Colin Simms wrote many poems from his personal experience on the trail of the vanishingly scarce pine martens surviving in the fells and dales of northern England in the mid to late twentieth century. In his 1973 book *Pine Marten, seven prints* – a mix of poetry and prose – Simms describes some of his encounters and the conservation issues faced by his 'marts' in the North Country, where the species was so rare that most authorities had declared it extinct (his subsequent book of poems *Otters and Martens*, published in 2004 by Shearsman Books, is also worth a read). His opening text is prescient:

> In the wild we will not see them much until we have transformed our terrorism into what they can trust. We have acquired them before, for their pelts: when they were prized as prime fur-bearers... This is a book for the closing of eyes to the traditional view that this animal was for its fur, for us, but has now left us. The marten survives; and courts our attention with charms and skills we have only to learn to appreciate again, and the marten will get to know us as contemporary and companion, perhaps... This is for the opening of the eyes, eventually, on new relationships.

Over forty years on, Simms's wishes are, thankfully, being realised: for today pine martens are widely appreciated for their charm and beauty – although there are still some hearts and minds to win over. They now feature in our culture in ways related to their appeal as wild animals to be enjoyed alive and free, rather than solely for their monetary value as fur-bearers or for their pest status in the eyes of game shooters and poultry-keepers. In Scotland there is a Pine Marten Bar at Glenmore in the Cairngorms National Park; at Torlundy in the Nevis Range near Fort William you can visit the Pine Marten Café; further south there is the tasty-sounding Pine Marten rotisserie pub-restaurant in East Lothian; and across the Highlands one can rent holiday cottages and lodges that advertise opportunities to view their martens on the premises. Even musicians are in on the act: *Pine Marten* is an innovative, Ireland-based, modern string band drawing on music from around the world; and *Pinemarten* is a Derbyshire-based composer and sound designer producing '80s inspired electronica with a human touch...'.

In modern literature, a pet pine marten called Psipsina features in Louis de Bernière's 1994 novel *Captain Correli's Mandolin* set on the Greek island of Cephalonia during the Second World War (the pedant in me has to point out that pine martens do not occur on the island – but stone martens do, so I suggest that Psipsina was probably a stone marten!). In Philip Pullman's *His Dark Materials* – a trilogy of fantasy novels published between 1995 and 2000 – the child Lyra has a dæmon called Pantalaimon that changes his form according to her quick-shifting imagination; but as Lyra approaches puberty Pan settles on the form of a pine marten, elegant and flowing to reflect the grace of the grown-up Lyra.

There is even a pine marten connection for the fans of J. K. Rowling's *Harry Potter* series of books about the adventures of a young trainee wizard and his friends. When faced with danger the young wizards wave their wands and shout *'Patronus'* in order to perform a complex and powerful defensive spell. The Patronus Charm takes the form of a creature linked to the particular witch or wizard performing the spell: in Harry Potter's case his Patronus is a stag and Hermione's is an otter. In September 2016 J. K. Rowling revealed to fans that her Patronus is a pine marten, saying she was happy because her fondness for weaselly creatures is well documented.

Pine martens have featured on postage stamps in many countries: in

Ireland in 1992, a World Wildlife Fund collection of four stamps featured paintings of pine martens; in the UK in 1986, a pine marten was on one of four 'species at risk' postage stamps designed by Ken Lilly, and a photograph of a pine marten was included in the UK's 2004 Woodland Animals commemorative stamp collection designed by Kate Stephens; and images of pine martens have appeared on postage stamps produced in Romania, Hungary, Moldova, Bulgaria, Belarus and Switzerland. However, there is no postal service more helpful to the struggling mammologist than Kazakhstan's: in 2016, it produced a delightful pair of postage stamps showing a pine marten and a stone marten, each thoughtfully illustrated within its preferred habitat of trees and rocks respectively.

To many naturalists and wildlife photographers, the quest to observe and photograph a wild pine marten is the focus for trips to the wilder parts of Britain and Ireland. There are well-established viewing hides, especially in the Scottish Highlands, where pine martens visit to feast on the bait provided while stunning images are captured. Unsurprisingly, images of an agile pine marten have twice won The Mammal Society's Mammal Photographer of the Year: by Maurice Flynn in 2015 and by Alastair Marsh in 2017.

ORIGINS AND CLOSE RELATIVES

The Weasel Family
Pine martens belong to the Mustelidae – the fabulously diverse weasel family – that has conquered land, rivers, sea and (almost) air around the globe. The Mustelidae is the largest and most diverse family in the order Carnivora: its members vary in body size nearly one thousand-fold, from the tiny weasel *Mustela nivalis* up to the hefty sea otter *Enhydra lutris*. The mustelids display an equally wide variety of lifestyles: the family includes tough bruisers like the solitary wolverine *Gulo gulo* that reigns supreme in the Arctic tundra where it scavenges the kills of wolves and polar bears; the slim stoats and weasels that pursue small rodents and lagomorphs down their burrows; strikingly marked polecats and their relatives that have staked their reputation on a pungent defence against predators; fossorial badgers that live in clans and feed on earthworms; giant river otters that hunt in packs along Brazilian rivers; colonial sea otters that harvest molluscs from the sea bed; and, finally, the arboreal martens that spend part of their lives above ground level.

Early origins and evolutionary history
The pine marten belongs to a group of attractive, mainly woodland-dwelling and medium-sized (roughly 1–2 kilograms in weight, though one or two are a bit bigger) members of the weasel family in the genus *Martes*. According to the fossil record and genetic evidence the genus *Martes* arose in moist tropical forests somewhere in south-west Eurasia during the early and middle Miocene; they diverged from other mustelids around 12 million years ago. Since then, the evolving *Martes* gang dispersed and speciated into its current form in response to changing climates, shifting geographical barriers and glacial events. Today all members of the *Martes* genus have retained their Miocene ancestor's association with woodland and trees, so this makes them all vulnerable to human activities that remove, fragment or degrade their favoured habitat.

Through the Miocene (23 to 5.3 million years before present (myBP)) and Pliocene (5.3 to 2.6 myBP) the fossil record reveals that ancestors of our modern *Martes* were subject to occasional 'turnover events' (episodes of geographic isolation lead to extinction or speciation) triggered by major environmental trauma such as sea level change, continental collisions and the appearance of new mountain ranges. Latterly, the onset of the first northern hemisphere glaciation towards the end of the Pliocene coincides approximately with the appearance of two fossil forms of *Martes* in central Europe: *M. wenzensis* and *M. filholi*.

According to a new synthesis of *Martes*' evolutionary history by Susan Hughes of the Pacific Northwest National Laboratory, the first glacial advance around 3.2 myBP marked the beginning of a long period of fluctuating climatic and habitat conditions for *Martes* species that must have triggered new adaptations and speciation through the Pleistocene (2.6 to 0.012 myBP). Each glacial phase would have forced the subtropical martens into warm refugia in southern Europe, where isolation created the genetic bottlenecks that eventually led to the adaptive changes, about 1.8 million years ago, enabling martens to radiate across northern Eurasia where cool temperate forests were establishing. According to Hughes' synthesis, in Europe around this time martens are represented by *Martes vetus*, which appeared in the fossil record between 1.8 and 0.4 million years ago, and by a larger form of *Martes martes*, which appeared about 0.12 million years ago.

The *Martes* Complex

Today there are eight *Martes* species, of which only two are found in Europe: the pine marten and the stone or beech marten *Martes foina*; and only the pine marten is naturally found in the wild in Britain and Ireland (although there is debate about whether the stone marten might have occurred in Britain and Ireland during historical times – I shall consider this below). The eight martens have several features in common: they tend to have rich, soft fur that is highly valued by humans for making clothes, especially in those species that inhabit cold climates – the so-called 'Boreal martens'; they have long, slim bodies with long tails; they are agile climbers that tend to rest and breed in tree cavities or equivalent elevated dens; and they have a reproductive system based upon a long period of delayed implantation. The long, slim body shape tends to influence the way martens move, typically involving an arched-back walk and a bounding lope; it also helps martens to squeeze into small spaces, such as the burrows and nests of their prey, as well as into subnivean tunnels on the wintry woodland floor.

Fisher
(Pekania pennanti) Pacific marten (Martes caurina) American marten (Martes americana) Wolverine (Gulo gulo) Pine marten (Martes martes) Wolverine (Gulo gulo) Sable (Martes zibellina)

Tayra (Eira barbara) Stone or beech marten (Martes foina) Nilgiri marten (Martes gwatkinsii) Yellow-throated marten (Martes flavigula) Japanese marten (Martes melampus)

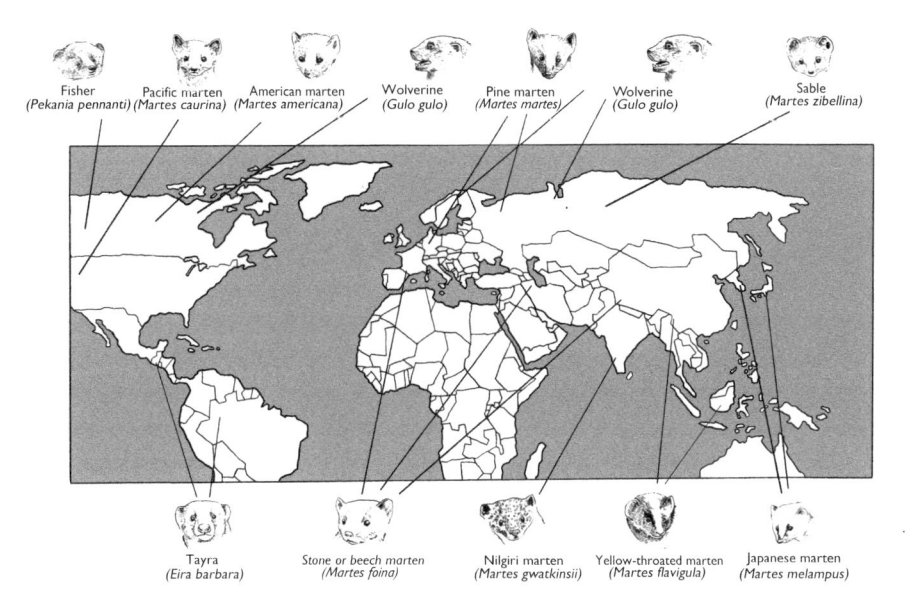

The eleven members of the 'Martes Complex' occupy many parts of the globe except Africa and Australia.

Five of the eight *Martes* species are distributed continuously around the globe in the teeth-chatteringly cold northern Boreal Forest zone, with a size gradient from the largest in Western Europe to the smallest in North America: these comprise the pine marten in western Eurasia; the sable *Martes zibellina* from Russia's Ural Mountains eastward to Japan; the Japanese marten *Martes melampus* in Japan; the Pacific marten *Martes caurina* in south-western USA; and the American marten *Martes americana* in the rest of the northern USA and parts of southern Canada (the last two have only recently been recognised as separate species). These five northern martens may be considered as a 'circumpolar super-species' with a probable common ancestor and a tendency to hybridise where their distributions overlap – for example, pine martens have been reported as hybridising with both the sable and American marten.

Further south there are three other martens that occupy the temperate and tropical zones. These 'milder martens' comprise the stone marten *Martes foina* and the closely related yellow-throated marten *Martes flavigula* and Nilgiri marten *Martes gwatkinsii*. The fur of these three species has been less highly valued because it is less dense than that of their cold-adapted Boreal relatives.

Beyond the Genus *Martes* there are three larger species, each the sole member of its own Genus, that are loosely related to the martens within what the Martes Working Group (the MWG – a friendly international bunch formed in 1993 to facilitate communication among scientists with a common interest in *Martes* research, conservation and management) calls 'The *Martes* Complex'. These comprise the fisher *Pekania pennanti*, the wolverine *Gulo gulo*, and the tayra *Eira barbara*. The fisher was originally classed as a *Martes* until recent studies confirmed it as a more distant relative. Regardless of any genetic evidence, in my view there are grounds for excluding it from the *Martes* Genus for sheer un-marten-like behaviour, for the fisher is a big bruiser that lacks the gentle martens' delicate finesse, and it kills porcupines as a hobby.

The eleven members of The Martes Complex

English name	Latin name	Distribution	IUCN Conservation Status and population trend
Pine marten	*Martes martes*	Western Eurasia	Least Concern Stable
Stone or beech marten	*Martes foina*	Western Eurasia (more southerly than pine marten), Himalayas, Mongolia and China	Least Concern Stable
Sable	*Martes zibellina*	Russia through China to Japan and Korea	Least Concern Increasing

Yellow-throated marten	*Martes flavigula*	South-east Asia	Least Concern Decreasing
Nilgiri marten	*Martes gwatkinsii*	South-west India	Vulnerable Stable
Japanese marten	*Martes melampus*	Japan and Korea	Least Concern Stable
American marten	*Martes americana*	Parts of northern and western USA and Canada	Least Concern Decreasing
Pacific marten	*Martes caurina*	Western United States and south-west Canada	As for *M. americana*
Fisher	*Pekania pennanti*	Canada and parts of northern and south-western USA	Least Concern Unknown
Wolverine	*Gulo gulo*	Canada, Scandinavia and Siberia, and parts of western USA	Least Concern Decreasing
Tayra	*Eira barbara*	Much of Central and South America	Least Concern Decreasing

Below we introduce the pine marten's closest relatives – the seven other members of the *Martes* Genus – in more detail. We know quite a lot about some of them; but a few of them are rather under-studied so there is still much to learn. There is a lot to say about the stone marten because it is found close to our islands on the European continent, where it is well studied, makes quite a nuisance of itself and is sometimes confused with the pine marten.

Stone Marten

The stone or beech marten is superficially very similar in size, shape, colour and behaviour to our pine marten, and the ranges of the two species overlap extensively on the European continent, so non-naturalists sometimes get them muddled up. For the sharp-eyed observer, however, there are some useful distinguishing features that help us to separate them: while both have brown fur and a large pale bib on the chest and throat, in the pine marten the bib has a tint that ranges from creamy through yellowish to apricot, while in the stone marten it is pure white. There are also differences in the extent and pattern of the bib, with the stone marten's tending to extend further down its chest on to the top of the front legs, where the white fur is often divided by a variable blob or 'finger' of brown fur projecting up from the lower chest; and there is a difference in the colour of the animals' soft woolly underfur, which is grey in the pine marten and whitish in the stone marten.

There are other minor differences that are less easy to spot unless you are able to examine both species in close-up: the stone marten has proportionally shorter legs and, associated with its more strictly nocturnal lifestyle, larger eyes than the pine marten. Other differences are summarised in the table opposite.

Despite their physical similarities, genetic evidence indicates that the pine marten is much less closely related to the stone marten than to the sable and American marten. Pine and stone martens reportedly separated into distinct species around 3.1 to 2.2 million years ago and there are no reports of hybridisation between the two, despite the many opportunities in their extensively overlapping geographical distributions.

Beyond their minor morphological differences, there are contrasts in behaviour and habitat use that explain how pine and stone martens can coexist over large parts of Europe (more on this below): stone martens choose to occupy more urban or human-modified habitats than do pine martens, which prefer extensive, near-natural woodlands. Using their special climbing skills and avoiding human detection by being strictly nocturnal, stone martens live like high-level urban foxes in many continental European towns and cities, resting in roof-top dens by day and descending to the streets at night to forage for fruit, small rodents and discarded human food. Of all the martens, the stone marten is the

Pine Marten *Martes martes*	Stone Marten *Martes foina*
Ears large and fringed with pale fur	Ears smaller with less colour contrast
Bib creamy-yellow to apricot; typically blotched and spotted with brown fur	Bib pure white; divides at lower end and extends on to the tops of the front legs
Rhinarium dark brown	Rhinarium pinkish brown
Guard hairs reddish brown; darker brown in summer	Guard hairs paler brown
Underfur grey	Underfur off-white
Underside of paws quite furry, especially in winter	Underside of paws not very furry
External face of 3rd upper premolar concave	External face of 3rd upper premolar convex
Average baculum length 46 mm	Average baculum length 60 mm

The main physical differences between the pine marten and stone marten (with thanks to Jean-François Noblet) only one to have adapted fully to live in truly urban environments, so in that sense its future is assured if we humans continue to build houses on European countryside.

Away from urban areas, stone martens live around villages and farmsteads in quite open countryside, where they typically rest and breed in the roofs of barns and farmhouses. This can lead to conflict with the human occupants who resent the noise and occasional smells coming through their bedroom ceilings, the theft of fruit from their gardens and the fresh dung left thoughtfully on window ledges, handrails and doorsteps. Owners of holiday homes in France often have reasons to curse *La Fouine* (also the name of a French rap group) because of the mess and mayhem waiting to greet them on their infrequent visits to de-stress in their rural retreats.

My only encounter with a wild stone marten was late on a summer's night in 2014 near the centre of the beautiful Polish city of Krakow (where the MWG held its International Symposium that year). We had been tipped off about the location on a quiet side-street by marten researcher Izabela Wierzbowska, so we loitered on the pavement like reluctant prostitutes while the good folk of Krakow passed us by on their way to and from the tempting nightspots around the city's central square. Our embarrassment was worthwhile, however, for at about 11.30 p.m. a long, low, furry figure drifted noiselessly along the pavement towards us, diving beneath the parked cars if ever a pedestrian or vehicle approached. Checking the litter-bins for discarded pizza, the stone marten worked its way along the street to a point where it climbed a tightly pruned urban tree, ran along the top of a high wall and descended into the churchyard beyond. It was a magical moment, and I especially remember the pure, light-footed silence of the marten, against the city's background hum, as it ghosted along the street using the parked cars as cover whenever danger threatened.

Talking of cars, since the late 1970s the stone marten has gained a reputation for nocturnal attacks on parked cars in towns and cities across central-western Europe. Known as the *auto-marder* (German) or *auto-marter* (Dutch) phenomenon, this involves the chewing of rubber-coated cables and coolant hoses and damage to noise and heat insulation material in the engine compartment of vehicles; they also chew other car parts such as external radio aerials. It was first reported from Switzerland in about 1978 and has since spread widely across the continent, leading to expensive and sometimes dangerous mechanical failure for thousands of drivers each year. In Germany alone, an estimated 160,000 cars are damaged each year at an annual cost of over two million Euros.

Why do they do it? The most plausible explanation – apart from malicious eco-terrorism (and we surely do need rescuing from our car-dependent transport system, but perhaps not this way) – is that the cosy, above-ground spaces beneath a car bonnet represent safe resting sites for stone martens, albeit the insulation needs a bit of rearranging to make it more comfortable, and the warm, rubber-coated cables carrying electric wires, coolant and brake fluid are tempting for a playful chew before one snuggles down for a nap. Another suggestion is that cable-chewing is the equivalent of worry-beads or cigarettes for the stressed urban stone marten chilling out after a night on the streets. Also plausible is the idea that, once a stone marten has left its scent beneath the bonnet of a car, if it is later parked elsewhere in the territory of different martens they will attack the engine compartment because it carries the scent of an 'invader'.

In response to the huge cost and inconvenience of stone marten damage to cars, there has been a flurry of research and development in the field of repellent methods among major car manufacturers (one even changed the chemical formula of its brake hoses to make them less appealing) and independent companies. For example, Mercedes offers a sophisticated three-function *Marderschutzanlage* (marten protection) system for its car engine compartments that aims to repel stone martens with a combination of high-voltage electric shocks, ultrasound and flashing lights. There are low-tech measures available, including parking on a wire mesh grid (which the martens apparently don't like to walk on), fitting wire mesh or cardboard barriers at ground level around the sides of parked cars, and installing a ticking clock, unwanted perfume or an old sock full of dog hair inside the engine compartment. If all this fails there is an assortment of commercially available *anti-marder* sprays, one of which is labelled 'Get Lost Marder!'

The stone marten's urban predilections and cable-chewing habits sometimes land it in the limelight in other bizarre ways: In March 2013, a stone marten stopped a Swiss League football match between FC Thun and Zurich when it performed a lone mustelid pitch invasion and evaded capture for more than five minutes. Wrongly labelled a pine marten in the popular YouTube footage (www.youtube.com/watch?v=45FoC7PqyJc), the terrified animal was filmed as it desperately tried to find a way off the pitch to safety, and even bit one of the Zurich defenders, Loris Benito, who foolishly caught it without gloves. And in April 2016 a stone marten – identified only as a 'weasel' in English language news reports but as a '*fouine*' in Swiss ones

– damaged the Large Hadron Collider at Cern in Switzerland by chewing through an electric cable carrying 66,000 volts; sadly it lost its life in the process.

The names 'stone' and 'beech' are both used by English speakers to identify *Martes foina*, although in my experience the former is now the most frequently used.

Sable

Similar in size and appearance to the pine marten, the sable has a more thickly-furred face and ears, a proportionately shorter tail and a less distinctive pale patch on its chest. Across its huge geographic range, there are some variations in body colour between light and dark brown; and the throat patch varies between white, grey and pale yellow. For many centuries, the sable has been the most highly prized fur-bearer in the marten clan because, in its winter pelage, it has extremely dense, soft, silky fur that enables it to thrive in the very low temperatures of a Siberian winter (its range extends up above the Arctic Circle). Apparently sable paint brushes, which are popular among water colour artists, are actually made from hairs taken from the tail of the Kolinsky *Mustela sibirica* – a weasel found in Siberia.

Sables were intensively harvested for their fur over vast areas of their Russian range in the nineteenth and early twentieth centuries, with subsequent reintroductions and legal protection to help populations recover. Now most sable fur is produced by captive animals reared on fur farms. The sable's huge value to the Russian economy earned it a prominent role in the 1981 Cold War crime novel *Gorky Park* by Martin Cruz Smith, which was adapted for a 1983 film (unexpectedly starring some pine martens) of the same name by English screenwriter Dennis Potter. The story follows an investigation of the gruesome murder in Moscow's Gorky Park of an American and two young Russians in connection with their attempt to smuggle six sables out of the country and so to break the Soviet monopoly on their valuable fur. The closing sequence of the film shows Arkady Renko (played by William Hurt) releasing the 'sables' from their cages; but as they bolt across the snow to the safety of the nearby woodland it is clear to me that they are not sables but pine martens. This deceitful piece of casting (doubtless spotted by only a few mustelid-nerds like me) is understandable because of Cold War access restrictions in place at the time: the film was actually shot in Scandinavia – with Helsinki standing in for Moscow – where pine martens would be more readily available because sables no longer occur there in the wild; and in any case, captive sables would have been far too valuable to release in front of the cameras.

Like most other martens the sable is omnivorous, preying on mammals such as hares and small rodents as well as birds and fruit; they also follow the tracks of wolves and bears to scavenge the remains of their kills of larger mammals. Sables inhabit the extensive Taiga forests, where they prefer the late successional stages with large diameter trees and abundant standing deadwood. The western part of their range overlaps with the pine marten in the Ural Mountains, where there are reports of hybridisation between these two closely related species. The hybrid offspring of interbreeding between a pine marten and sable is known in Russian as a *kidas*, and these are reported to behave in ways that maintain 'reproductive isolation' (scientist-speak for being unusually fussy or frigid during the mating season). As a consequence, the already low reproductive rate of both pine martens and sables drops even further where hybridisation occurs, leading to suggestions that this acts as an effective barrier to more extensive range overlap and further hybridisation between the two species.

Yellow-throated marten
This rather different-looking marten has a wide distribution centred on South East Asia, where it occupies an extraordinary diversity of environments from tropical and temperate forests to much colder subalpine and alpine regions. Nevertheless, it seems appropriate that this mainly tropical species is the most brightly coloured and strikingly marked of all the martens, with a dark brownish-black head, white lower lips and chin and a body colour that grades from yellow-orange on the throat and chest through yellow flanks and belly and darker brown hindquarters to its very long and shiny black tail (which is longer than the body); the feet and lower legs are dark brown or black. With males weighing up to 5 kilograms, yellow-throated martens are the biggest of the Old World martens; and their fur is shorter and less fluffy than the more cold-adapted martens. The males have an unusual S-shaped baculum (penis bone) with

four blunt knobs on its tip, the purpose of which we can only guess at.

Yellow-throated martens are robust and fearless, and use their anal scent glands to produce a rather un-marten-like defensive stink (their striking colour may serve to warn potential predators of this pungent defence). They are diurnal, omnivorous and typically hunt in small gangs of two to six individuals; this enables them to tackle surprisingly large prey such as musk deer, Chinese water deer, Langur monkeys and the young of larger ungulates and wild boar; they may even follow tigers in the hope of sneaking bits of their kills; and yellow-throated martens consume a wide range of fruit when it is seasonally abundant, so they may have a role as seed dispersers in tropical forest ecosystems.

There is still a lot to learn about yellow-throated martens: in a recent review, the Martes Working Group concluded that there is little information on its population status and trends, although the species is considered to be rare. We also know little about its habitat associations, breeding biology, food habits and general behaviour. Unlike most of their polygamous relatives, yellow-throated martens are reported to be monogamous.

Not surprisingly, given their rather different appearance, behaviour, social lives and reproductive systems, both the yellow-throated and Nilgiri marten (see below) are rather distant – genetically speaking – from other *Martes* species, so they have been assigned to their own subgenus called Charronia.

Nilgiri marten

The Nilgiri marten is similar in appearance and closely related to the yellow-throated marten – until recently the two were considered to be the same species – but is smaller and less brightly coloured: its head and body are covered in very dark brown fur with a bright yellow-orange chest. Found in the wooded country of the Nilgiri Hills and Western Ghats of southern India, no other marten species occupies such a small global distributional range. That is one reason why the Nilgiri marten is the only one classed as vulnerable to extinction by the IUCN. It is believed to be threatened by habitat loss and disturbance in the moist tropical forests it inhabits, despite the fact that much of its patchy distribution coincides with protected areas. Like the yellow-throated marten there is very little known about this animal, and the lack of basic information on ecology and behaviour is a cause for great concern; and like its close relative above, the Nilgiri marten is said to be diurnal and monogamous.

Japanese marten
Another quite brightly coloured and rather cute-looking fluffy marten, the Japanese marten has an off-white face and a pale body that varies between creamy-yellow and orange in different individuals; and some are brownish on the body and face. These colour variations coincide with the three subspecies recognised in Japan. This marten is strongly associated with forests and avoids modern plantations and open fields. Japanese martens are still trapped and killed for their attractive fur over most of their range. The species is also threatened by logging and conversion of broadleaved forests to coniferous plantations. There is an urgent need to improve knowledge of Japanese marten ecology and behaviour, to monitor populations and improve management of harvesting for fur, and to establish protected areas where populations can be conserved.

American marten
Slightly confusingly, Americans and Canadians sometimes refer to their marten as 'the pine marten', although this is forgivable because *Martes americana* looks quite similar to our European pine marten and we know that the two are so closely related that they can interbreed. American martens can be quite colourful, especially in winter pelage when the delicate grey fur on the head and ears contrasts with an orangey-brown body, dark brown legs and tail and a cream, yellow or bright orange chest patch.

The American marten has been studied more intensively than any other because of its value as a fur-bearer that is still harvested by trapping over much of its range, and because of the need to minimise the impacts of both fur-trapping and commercial timber harvesting upon its populations. Consequently, most research has concentrated upon monitoring population status via detection surveys – traditionally based upon counting marten tracks in snow, but now augmented by camera trapping – to ensure that trapping is conducted at sustainable levels.

More recently, studies have focused upon the American marten's ecology and habitat associations in order to inform forest management plans. Of course, it helps that the American marten occupies two of the world's wealthiest countries – Canada and the USA – that can afford to pay for such research more easily than other countries.

Thanks to well-funded and sensibly directed research, the American marten's conservation needs are better understood than is the case for most of the other martens. However, this does not guarantee it a secure future where commercial priorities are sometimes dominant. The IUCN classes the American marten as 'Decreasing', and south of its main Canadian range, protected populations are small and fragmented and their status is not well known. Notably, studies have identified a serious conflict of interest because the martens show a clear preference for living in the same mature, closed-canopy forest stands, with large diameter trees and high volumes of coarse woody debris, that are most attractive to the timber harvesters. Although marten populations in much of Canada appear stable, despite annual harvests in Quebec and Ontario of around 30,000, there are concerns about habitat degradation and increased trapping associated with construction of new access routes into wilderness areas to facilitate oil and gas exploration.

Pacific marten

Recent genetic and morphometric studies of North American martens previously all classed as *Martes americana* have prompted a taxonomic rethink in respect of animals occupying the western parts of North America (basically all the western United States and parts of British Columbia). These martens are now reclassified as a distinct species known as the Pacific marten *Martes caurina*. Like its close relative the American marten, this species shows a preference for mature 'old growth' forests that are extensive and undisturbed by timber harvesting.

Pine marten history, genetics and distribution in Europe

At the height of the last Ice Age some 18,000 years ago, conditions in Britain and Ireland were too severe for pine martens to survive so, in keeping with most other mammals, populations had to bide their time in the warmer, ice-free parts of Europe until the ice sheets retreated.

The distribution of fossil pine martens around this time suggests that the species occupied several different refugia, although this is contradicted by genetic sampling of modern pine martens from specimens across Europe: Angus Davison and colleagues studied pine marten phylogeography – the pattern of a species' ancient distributional change – and concluded from the low level of genetic variability that pine marten populations present today in northern and central Europe had spread from just one or two refugia somewhere in central-southern Europe – probably between the Pyrenees and Romania – after the glaciation came to an end.

However, a more recent and wider study by Aritz Ruiz-González and colleagues suggests that pine marten phylogeography is more complicated, including contributions from animals lurking in cryptic (previously unidentified) northern glacial refugia. The Ruiz-González analysis revealed three main genetic groupings that correspond broadly to glacial refugia identified as Mediterranean, Central Northern European and Fennoscandia-Russian. In contrast to the Davison study above, the Ruiz-González study concluded that the Mediterranean group contributed rather little to the pine marten's rapid recolonisation of Eurasia after the ice sheets retreated; instead recolonisation was fuelled mainly by animals from the Central Northern European group, which included some cryptic northern glacial refugia.

The genetic diversity of pine marten populations across the species' range is indicated by the number and distribution of haplotypes (this term is a contraction of the phrase 'haploid genotype', which refers to a particular combination of genetic markers used to identify and characterise populations, so a haplotype is simply a genetically distinctive strain within a species or subspecies). The Ruiz-González study identified 69 different haplotypes among the 287 pine marten specimens sampled from 21 countries. Just three of those haplotypes are known to occur today in Britain and Ireland: these are known as Haplotypes *a*, *i* and *p*.

The pine martens found in Ireland today are all of haplotype *p*, whereas in Scotland, Wales and England only haplotypes *a* and *i* occur. However, this was not always the case: up until the early 1900s Irish pine martens were predominantly of haplotype *i*, which is the same as that found historically in England and Wales. Haplotype *i* was last found in Ireland in a pine marten dating from 1912, and it seems to have been replaced by haplotype *p* (first found in a 1915 specimen), which is presumed to have evolved directly from its predecessor that then died out in Ireland during the era of heavy human persecution in the early 1900s. Today, all Irish pine martens apparently are of haplotype *p*.

The historical co-occurrence of haplotype *i* in England, Wales and Ireland supports the view that today's Irish martens originally came from mainland (southern) Britain, but it is not clear whether they took themselves across one of the land bridges linking the islands as the last Ice Age fizzled out; or whether pine martens were imported to Ireland by early human settlers travelling across the Irish Sea from Wales (the lack of early archaeological evidence of martens in Ireland would tend to support the latter scenario). Furthermore, because haplotype *i* also occurs in Iberia, it is possible that the martens in Ireland and southern Britain originated from the Mediterranean glacial refugium, with northern Britain colonised by martens of a different haplotype from somewhere like Scandinavia.

On the British mainland, there were two pine marten haplotypes present historically: haplotype *i* in Wales and England, and both haplotype *i* and *a* in Scotland (although here haplotype *a* was apparently always dominant numerically); haplotype *i* was last found in England from a specimen dated 1924; and the last haplotype *i* in Wales was from a specimen from 1950. Despite intensive searching by The Vincent Wildlife Trust and others, nobly led by Neil Jordan, no further evidence of haplotype *i* has been found in Wales or England; in fact, all of the contemporary pine marten specimens south of the Scottish border have been of haplotype *a* (suggesting a Scottish origin) or occasionally of continental haplotypes (suggesting release or escape from captivity of pine martens imported from continental Europe or the descendents thereof).

Thus, it seems that the historical haplotype *i* was lost from Ireland, Wales and England during the twentieth century, which would suggest that pine martens of that haplotype were genetically disadvantaged in some way in the face of heavy human persecution; and perhaps they still are in modern times? The VWT's Pine Marten Recovery Project has recently translocated animals of haplotype *a* from Scotland to Wales (with further Scottish translocations to the Forest of Dean likely in the near future), so we should expect that apparently better-adapted haplotype to predominate in southern Britain from now on. Haplotype *i* is still present –

though rare – in Scotland, based on two live specimens recovered in 2010 from an island in the west of the country. Surely haplotype *i* still occurs elsewhere in Scotland; and could there even be other British haplotypes just waiting to be discovered in some remote glen or strath? Thankfully, a wide-scale genetic assessment of pine marten populations is currently under way in Ireland and Britain, so I expect we will learn much more about the distribution of haplotypes in the near future.

Pine marten range   Stone marten range

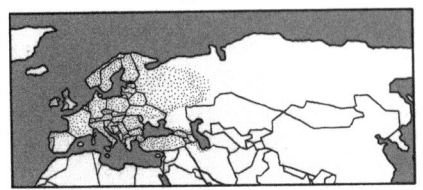

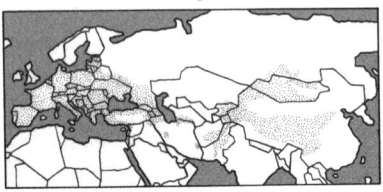

The pine marten has a more northerly distribution than the less cold-adapted stone marten, which occurs much further south-east into Asia.

Pine martens have been introduced on to some offshore islands where the scarcity or absence of competitors and predators enables them to behave in unusual ways. For example, on the Mediterranean island of Menorca pine martens occupy a wide range of habitats with no obvious preference for trees and woodland.

Is the stone/beech marten native to the British Isles?
The conventional view is that, in common with some other European mammals, the stone or beech marten did not make it across to Britain or Ireland before the English Channel formed following the last Ice Age, so we should not regard it as a native animal that was exterminated at some point in pre-history by our ancestors. This position is supported by the apparent absence of fossil or more recent skeletal remains of stone martens (though these are difficult to separate from those of pine martens), as well as the apparent absence of preserved skins or mounted specimens (although fading of old skins would also make separation difficult in the absence of genetic analysis). Further support comes from the suggestion that the stone marten was probably absent from Western Europe in the Late Glacial period and, even if this was not the case, its

lack of adaptation to cold climates means that it would have been slow to spread north from its cosy glacial refuge on the Eurasian continent.

An alternative view is that, prior to the late 1800s, naturalists clearly recognised two types of marten in Britain, sometimes identified as the 'white-breasted' and 'yellow-breasted' (although a variety of other names were used to separate them in both Welsh and English). For example, in the Victoria County History of my own county of Worcestershire (published in 1901) Tomes writes: 'It is doubtful if the white-breasted marten has been found in the county for many years if at all, no record of it exists; but I can however speak of the yellow-breasted as having been killed more than half a century since at Falke Mill near Evesham'. In a more authoritative and comprehensive treatise entitled *A History of British Animals* by John Fleming, published in 1828, the two species are described as follows:

> *Martes fagorum.* Common Martin – Throat and breast white.
> The length of the body is about 18 inches, the tail 10. The general colour of the fur is dark brown, the head having a reddish tinge – it is a great destroyer of poultry and game. Easily tamed. Lodges frequently in hollows of trees, and brings forth from four to six young.
>
> *Martes abietum.* Pine-Martin – Throat and breast yellow.
> This species is somewhat less than the preceding; the colour of the fur is darker, and it is softer to the touch. It builds its nests in the tops of trees, and prefers wild situations, while the common sort approaches houses. The fur of this species, before the Union, formed a lucrative article of export from Scotland. The characters of these two species are ill defined.

Also writing in 1828 about both the pine and beech marten in his *Natural History of British and Foreign Quadrupeds,* James Hamilton Fennell asserts that 'The pine marten is more rare in Britain than the other sort, and in England neither is found except in the northern parts… The beech marten does sometimes, in the highlands of Scotland, where it is common and called *tuggin* [note this name is similar to *taghan* –

the modern Scottish Gaelic for pine marten], takes to killing lambs, and makes sad havoc. Luckily, however, it is nearly exterminated in the south of that country'. In the Lakeland fells, where 'marts' were commonly hunted with hounds, Macpherson reported in 1892 that old hunters used to recognise two types of marten – the 'Crag Mart' and the 'Pine Mart' – that differed in their colouration.

These are but three of several written references to the historical presence in Britain of two types of marten, with further authoritative statements spanning a hundred years, notably by Pennant (1768), Macgillivray (1833–43), Goldsmith (1840) and Bell (1874). Presumably the stone marten became extinct at some stage during the mid-1800s, enabling sceptics to argue that it had never occurred here (see below).

This view of two separate martens existing in the British Isles appears prevalent up to the point in 1879 when R. Alston published a paper in the Proceedings of the Zoological Society of London entitled *On the specific identity of the British Martens*. In his paper, Alston argued that sub-fossil evidence ruled out the presence of the stone marten, so any future references to martens in Britain and Ireland should use the name 'pine marten' only. Amazingly, considering the flimsy evidence base (there are not very many sub-fossil *Martes* specimens from the British Isles, and *foina* and *martes* skeletons are not easy to separate anyway), this firm dictat seems to have been widely accepted at the time, so there has been little mention of stone martens as a native species ever since. Subsequently, some authorities explained the presence of 'white breasted' martens as an age-related colour variation in the pine marten. For example, writing in 1950, Oliver Pike (a Fellow of the Zoological Society of London) states 'The breast... is a lovely bright orange, varying to pale cream to greyish white according to age. Our older naturalists placed this white variety as a different species, naming it the beech marten'. While this age-related fading of the breast fur is doubtless true of mounted taxidermy specimens exposed to daylight, in my experience it does not occur in live pine martens; in fact, I know of captive animals that lived to the age of 20 years and still wore rich, yellow-orange throat-patches after their biannual moult. I suspect there is much more to discover on this story, and friends and I have a cunning plan to explore the literature and museum specimens a bit further.

Stone martens have been kept in captivity in Britain in recent times, sometimes on fur farms. I remember meeting John Stevenson in the late 1970s, who had owned a mink farm on the edge of Dartmoor in the 1950s. He told me how he once 'lost' a captive stone marten from his collection and never saw it until nine years later it was found dying in a neighbour's barn less than a mile away. It had apparently lived out a lonely life in the wooded valley of the River Teign for all that time without arousing any interest among the locals.

Whether or not the stone marten was ever once resident here in the wild, given its willingness to explore and inhabit a variety of human-made structures, we cannot rule out the possibility that it may one day make its way through the channel tunnel that connects Kent to a part of northern France where stone martens are well established.

THE BODY BEAUTIFUL

Shape and movement

Among all the enchanting wild mammals that inhabit these islands the pine marten, for me, would win any beauty contest paws down. It has the good looks, charm and grace – the ultimate in *Mustelid chic* – to win over the harshest of judges (and I have no doubt it would be keen to travel and meet people, raise piles of money for charity and then settle down to open a beauty salon in a woodland near you). With its long, slim, sinuous body and busily alert demeanour, the pine marten is unmistakably a mustelid; but the long bushy tail, longish legs, prominent muzzle and forward-pointing ears offer delicate hints of a foxy or feline affinity. Alongside the streamlined, semi-aquatic otter and the chunky, fossorial badger, the pine marten is yet another variation on the mustelid theme, this time with a lean but strong-limbed body supporting arboreal rather than aquatic or subterranean aspirations.

There is a particular delicacy about the pine marten's movements: even on the ground it has a floaty, light-stepping style as if walking on hot coals; naturalist-poet Colin Simms perfectly described the slightly pigeon-toed walking gait of the front limbs as 'very deliberately and as if dribbling a ball between the legs'. A glance at the pine marten's skeleton offers some explanation for its buoyantly muscular grace, for it reveals a curious combination of delicate and robust structures: the pelvis and ribcage are surprisingly slight, and the scapulae (shoulder blades) are small, albeit with large ridges for muscle attachment; like an arboreal primate the limbs are disproportionately robust in comparison with the delicate spine, although there are long spinal processes in the lumbar and shoulder sections for muscle attachment; and the articulated bones of the hind feet are extraordinarily long and springy, measuring nearly 10 centimetres from heel to claws. Many of these skeletal features can be viewed as adaptations to a climbing lifestyle as we shall see below.

Starting at the front end, the pine marten has an exquisite, heart-shaped face that is dominated by the hunter's sensory armoury of hearing, smell and sight: pert, triangular, cat-like ears sit above a fine elongated muzzle tipped by a neat, brown *rhinarium* (the moist rubbery bit on the end); between the ears and muzzle are two of the beadiest browny-black eyes you will ever encounter – forward-pointing and apparently unblinking – they remind us that eyesight is a crucial sense for an agile, climbing mammal. Vibrissae (whiskers) project from the muzzle to a maximum length of some 70 millimetres. The pine marten's prominent ears are proportionately larger and more forward-pointing than those of our other mustelids, indicating their radar-like importance as a means to pinpoint accurately the rustling of small rodents and amphibians among leaf litter on the woodland floor.

Behind its head, the pine marten has the long, slim neck and body typical of the smaller mustelids. Like a flexible, furry tube, this body shape is perfect for exploring burrows, tree cavities, tunnels under snow and other restricted spaces in search of prey and safe resting sites. But as we shall see below, this long, slim body shape presents martens with problems during cold winter weather. Other elements of the pine marten's shape are related to its agile, climbing lifestyle, as we shall see in *Arboreal adaptations* below (see page 40).

Coping with the cold

Our pine marten belongs to the 'Boreal' group of martens that live in the cold northern forests where, because of their thermo-energetically inefficient slim body shape, their fur that is not exceptionally insulative and their lack of large fat reserves, they face energetic challenges during winter. The pine marten's basal metabolic rate has been calculated at 88.18 kilocalories per day, which is about 20 per cent higher than expected for a more standard mammal shape. The marten's less than ideal fur and the limited amount of subcutaneous fat compound their thermal inefficiency during low temperatures: this relatively poor insulation means that they have a higher thermal conductance (capacity for heat loss) than that predicted for animals of their size. Finally, because of their limited fat reserves and their inability to fast for long periods, martens are forced to forage on an almost daily basis, so they cannot avoid bouts of extremely cold weather by resting inside insulated dens for long periods.

Pine martens and their Boreal relatives cope with cold weather by decreasing their activity levels during winter. A study by Andrzej Zalewski of pine marten activity patterns in Białowieża Forest in eastern Poland showed that they reduced their total active time from an average of 12 hours per day in summer to just 2.8 hours per day in winter; this change was achieved by increasing the duration of resting periods as the ambient temperatures fell. As well as reducing winter heat loss by spending more time in cosy dens, the martens' lower winter activity enables them to save energy and cope with less food: a study of the closely related American martens by Jonathan Gilbert revealed that they reduced their energy expenditure and food requirements by 28 per cent in winter as a consequence of lowering their activity levels and their field metabolic rates.

Another strategy to reduce winter energy costs found in some Boreal martens is to shift towards more daytime foraging activity when the sun is up and temperatures are raised: this has been reported for American martens but not our European pine marten (perhaps because of the risks of disturbance or persecution by humans). Other winter strategies may involve resting in dens at or below ground level or beneath snow instead of high up trees (although this may involve greater predation risks); and foraging for larger prey that may be stored in food caches, which may be more efficient in cold weather than making frequent excursions to catch small prey.

Body size and sexual dimorphism
Pine martens are the largest of the small mustelids in Britain and Ireland,

so are bigger than stoats, weasels, mink and polecats – although there is some size overlap with polecats, which tend to be shorter but chunkier than pine martens. In line with other small mustelids, pine martens are sexually dimorphic, with males being significantly larger than females. Based on mean body weights, males are typically 1.42 times bigger than females. The tables below show body measurements for pine martens from eastern Poland, Scotland and Ireland. They reveal that here at the western extremity of their range our pine martens are significantly larger than the Polish ones; in fact female pine martens in Ireland and Scotland are, on average, as big as male Polish pine martens. Irish and Scottish pine martens are pretty similar in size, although on average the latter are a shade bigger according to the measurements below.

The pine marten's pattern of sexual dimorphism is common in small mustelids and is best explained by the different pressures facing each gender, especially in relation to mating and the rearing of young: being large helps males to compete with other males for access to females during the hurly-burly of the frantic mating season, and it also enables the males to catch and restrain the smaller females during the act itself; and females benefit from being small because it minimizes their energy needs and this enables them to divert a greater proportion of the energy acquired from the food they catch to their kits. One spin-off benefit of sexual size dimorphism is that foraging males and females tend to concentrate upon a slightly different size range of prey, which might reduce competition between them where their home ranges overlap.

Polish pine martens

	Males		Females	
Measurements	*n*	Mean	*n*	Mean
Body weight (kg)	23	1.36	17	0.96
Head + body length (cm)	18	46.0	15	41.3
Tail length (cm)	18	23.0	15	20.2

Measurements of adult pine martens from Białowieża Forest, Poland from 1961–2005 (with thanks to Andrzej Zalewski, Polish Academy of Sciences).

Scottish

	Males		Females	
Measurements	n	Mean (and range)	n	Mean (and range)
Body weight (kg)	22	1.93 (1.77–2.1)	18	1.36 (1.2–1.54)
Head + body length (cm)	22	52.02 (50.5–53)	18	47.05 (46–48)
Tail length (cm)	22	24.0 (22–26)	18	22.28 (20.5–24)

Measurements of adult pine martens live-trapped in the Scottish Highlands during autumns 2015 and 2016 (with thanks to Jenny Macpherson of the VWT).

Irish

	Males		Females	
Measurements	n	Mean (and range)	n	Mean (and range)
Body weight (kg)	11	1.82 (1.5–2.1)	5	1.42 (1.25–1.65)
Head + body length (cm)	11	47.1 (44.3–50.8)	5	42.5 (40.8–45.9)
Tail length (cm)	11	24.9 (22.3–29.2)	5	22.84 (21.2–24.3)

Measurements from adult road-casualty Irish pine martens collected during 2015 and 2016 from public roads in both Northern Ireland and the Republic (with thanks to Josh Twining of the University of Belfast).

Arboreal adaptations

The pine marten's most visible adaptation to a life of elevated climbing, leaping and balancing is its very long and bushy tail, which amounts to almost exactly half the length of its head and body. As well as helping the animal to balance during tricky arboreal manoeuvres, in winter the thickly furred tail provides extra insulation against low temperatures when wrapped around a sleeping marten in a tree-hole den. Away from the trees there is a suggestion, arising from a study of Pacific martens by Flaherty and colleagues, that the balancing effect of a long tail reduces the need for extreme dorsal spine flexing when the animal is bounding on the ground; and the 'whiplash' effect of a long tail may also boost stride length.

Next are the pine marten's powerful limbs, which are long and strong when compared with those of the other, more stumpy-legged mustelids: the marten's forelegs are especially muscular as an aid to safe and speedy climbing; even in quite young marten kits the forelimbs are well developed and capable of a powerful grip via their needle-sharp claws, presumably to prevent them from falling to the ground as they explore the limits of an elevated tree-hole natal den.

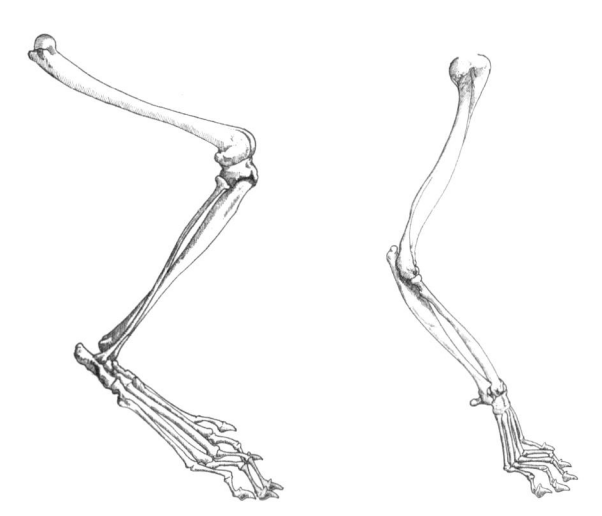

The pine marten's rear (left) and front (right) limb bones are long and robust, with springy metatarsal and metacarpal bones supporting the feet.

The strong, broad, five-toed feet are also important for climbing, and in pine martens the feet are surprisingly large in relation to the rest of the body: in an adult male, each front foot is typically 40–50 millimetres wide and long (excluding the proximal or heel pad). Although the undersides of the feet are well furred – especially in the winter coat – the small rubbery toe pads always remain prominent and fur-free on the front feet as an aid to gripping surfaces while climbing and the undersides of the hind feet are very furry in winter so their toe pads are partly concealed. More essential to the marten's grip while climbing, of course, are the pale, cat-like claws that are large, thick at the base, very sharp at the tips and markedly curved. Although not fully retractile like a cat's claws, the pine marten is able to adjust their position on its toes when no special grip is needed so that the tips are held above the substrate it walks on; this avoids them becoming worn or blunted in the way that a pet dog's claws do if it is walked mainly on hard surfaces.

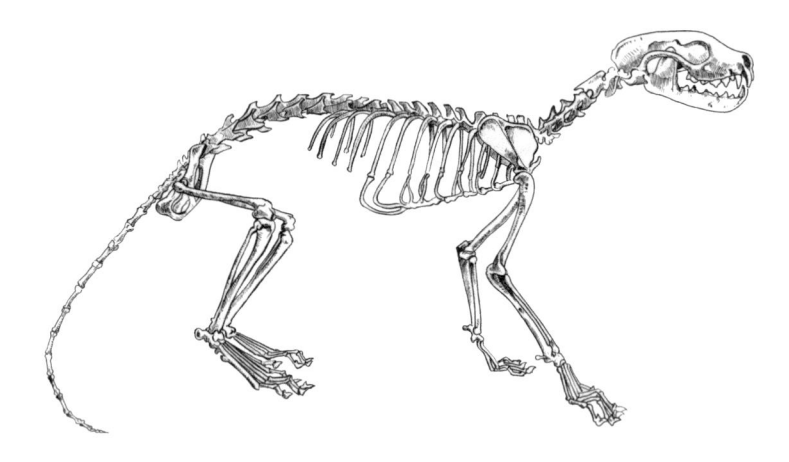

The pine marten's skeleton reflects the need for a high strength-to-bodyweight ratio in an arboreal mammal, with robust limbs contrasting with an otherwise lightweight build.

There is one special skeletal adaptation that helps to stop pine martens from falling to the ground prematurely as they climb down a tree: like dormice and squirrels, pine martens have remarkably flexible ankles on their hind feet; they can turn their hind feet through 180° as they descend, so that they can use their hind foot claws to grip in many different positions and thereby reduce the speed of their descent.

Finally, an adaptation found in many arboreal mammals is a high strength to body-weight ratio, which is essential if an animal needs to

PINE MARTENS | THE BODY BEAUTIFUL

Like squirrels and dormice, pine martens have flexible ankles on their hind feet, enabling them to turn them around as they descend a tree.

climb swiftly, leap with confidence and make use of slim branches that cannot bear heavy weights. This advantageous ratio is usually achieved by animals having bodily designs that avoid unnecessary bulk. The pine marten limits its bodyweight by having a relatively light-weight skeleton except for its limbs, which support the important climbing muscles. Pine martens also carry remarkably little body fat, which represents quite a sacrifice for an animal that inhabits the cold, northern forests where a thick layer of subcutaneous fat would add valuable insulation against low winter temperatures. On a more positive note, the pine marten's combination of a lightweight build and large, broad feet helps it to travel over – rather than to flounder through – the deep snow that still dominates northern parts of its range in winter.

Skull and teeth

In fully mature animals the pine marten's skull is topped by a modest saggital crest for the attachment of jaw muscles, although this is much less pronounced than in the badger's skull. Although less flattened, the marten's skull shape is similar to that of the much larger otter, with an elongated braincase, wide and delicate zygomatic arches, and the full complement of four premolars. There is a post-orbital constriction (or 'waist') but this is not so narrow as the otter's.

The pine marten's dentition is unmistakably carnivorous, with four

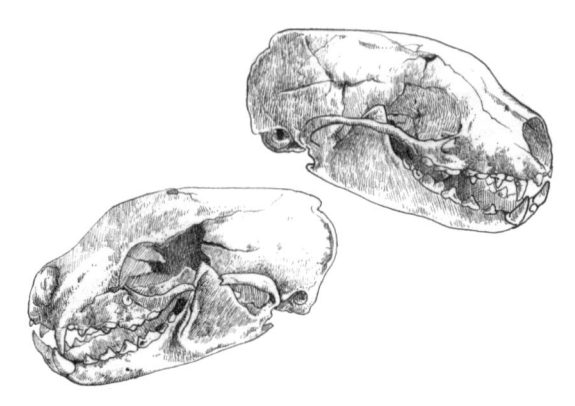

The skull of a young male pine marten, damaged when it was killed by a car on a minor road in mid-Wales in October 2012.

sharp canines at the front and an impressive row of cutting carnassials behind. There is a neat symmetry to the adult pine marten's dental formula, with each of the four tooth rows having three tiny incisors, one long, sharp canine, four premolars and two molars. The pine marten's dental formula is expressed as 2(I3/3 C1/1 P4/4 M2/2), which amounts to a total of 40 adult teeth; for comparison, the European polecat has only 34 adult teeth because it has four fewer premolars and two fewer molars.

In the days before wildlife research was closely regulated, biologists could remove a small tooth from a sedated pine marten in order to determine its age by creating wafer-thin cross sections of the root and counting the incremental growth rings in the cementum. Nowadays this approach is viewed as needlessly invasive, so kinder but less accurate ageing methods are used, such as the subjective assessment of tooth wear. Tooth wear is a fact of life for mammals that chew their food properly, and because the extent of wear generally increases with age this feature can be used by biologists to assign individuals to simple age categories (although detailed analysis by Sandrine Ruette of pine martens killed by trappers in France shows that this method is not perfect). Close scrutiny of a pine marten's teeth is only really possible when an animal is either dead or sedated, for example when one is immobilized to fit or remove a radio collar.

As part of the Pine Marten Recovery Project, the VWT used tooth wear assessment to categorise sedated Scottish martens as either young, middle-aged or old. Helpfully, their live-trapping was undertaken in September and October when juvenile pine martens – although almost adult-sized – could still be identified by their pristine coats, 'baby' faces and perfect, needle-sharp teeth. Their flawless dentition contrasted with that of older animals that had spent a few years chewing on field voles and other crunchy prey; older martens typically had a missing incisor or two, one or more broken canines, and noticeably blunted carnassials.

Teeth are so important for survival in carnivorous mammals such as pine martens that tooth wear is probably the dominant factor in determining how long they live in the wild. Once too many canines are broken or blunted their ability to catch and kill small rodents is severely constrained; and blunt carnassials are of little use when chewing on the tough, dry carcass of a wolf-killed deer.

Fur colour and moult

Pine martens have rich brown fur covering most of their bodies, which contrasts with a striking pale 'bib' on the throat and chest. Here I must confess to a guilty secret: I find a strangely edible quality in the pine marten's éclair-like combination of brown and creamy yellow, which suggests to me something wickedly delicious crafted by a top-class chocolatier. The colour of the body fur varies between individuals – some have a ginger or chestnut hue – and with the seasons. Pine martens moult twice a year: in spring the woolly winter fur is shed as the shorter summer coat grows through to replace it. In some animals, pale whispy remnant winter guard hairs linger on the body late into the summer to give them a slightly scruffy, unkempt appearance. In September, the winter fur starts to grow through to replace the summer coat, a process that is complete by mid-October.

In winter pelage, the longer, thicker winter fur is a medium gingery-brown, although on the legs and muzzle it is darker; in summer pelage, the body fur is a much darker brown so that, in the murky dusk, pine martens may appear almost black. In both pelage states the darkest fur tends to be on the lower legs and feet, where it contrasts with the pale cream claws (although some Scottish martens have small tufts of creamy fur on their toes). Also, sunlight may lead to a fading of fur on the dorsal surface of the body, so that in late summer adult martens have paler fur on their backs than on their undersides.

The pine marten's fur is made up of two types of hair: the long, glossy guard hairs that are relatively robust; and the soft underfur that is relatively short and woolly. The colour difference between the winter and summer coats is partly due to the greater influence of the grey underfur, which is longer and thicker in the winter pelage. Underfur colour is one useful way of distinguishing between pine and stone martens at close quarters, especially if one is examining the squashed remains of a road casualty and the differences in bib colour are not apparent, for example: in the pine marten, the underfur is always greyish; and in the stone marten it is a much lighter off-white colour.

The contrasting length and density of the pine marten's fur in its two pelage states has quite an impact on the animals' appearance: in their thin summer coats, they are reminiscent of giant big-eared stoats with sparsely bushy tails; and in winter they appear so much chunkier in their long thick fur that they look to me like miniature bushy-tailed bears.

Close inspection of a pine marten's face reveals a subtle pattern of brown and ginger shades, especially in the paler winter pelage, with the shortest, darkest fur on the muzzle and a hint of dark 'eyeliner' around the eyes. The prominent ears are fringed with short pale cream fur and partly filled with tufts of longer creamy fur. The muzzle is where the spring moult starts: in early April, the winter fur is shed first from around the nose and is replaced progressively by the darker summer fur, leaving a pronounced 'moult line' that moves steadily backwards towards the ears and beyond; by mid-May this moult line lies between the eyes and the ears, making some adult pine martens look as if they are wearing spectacles.

The pine marten's pale bib varies in colour from off-white in very young juveniles to a rich orangey-apricot colour in some recently moulted adults (bibs seem to fade after the moult, so their colours tend to be richest in early summer and autumn); in between these extremes bibs range in colour from pale cream through to a rich orangey-yellow. The bib typically starts about three or four centimetres behind the lower lip and extends all the way down the throat and on to the chest area between the front legs, where it tends to break up into patches or blotches of pale amongst the brown body fur. The bib is wide enough to occupy the whole of the ventral surface from the angle of the jaw below the ears down to the tops of the forelimbs. It is common to see spots, patches or 'fingers' of brown fur within the pale bib; these markings may be distinctive and unique, so can be helpful in identifying individual martens on camera trap images or at feeding stations.

Naturalists have noted some subtle differences between Irish and Scottish pine martens in the patterning and extent of the bib: in Scottish animals, it tends to extend further down the chest on to the area between the front legs; and in Irish martens the bib extends less far down and there is more 'blotchiness' towards its lower edge than in Scottish ones (I am grateful to Dave Tosh and Josh Twining for sharing their photos of Irish marten bibs). We should not be surprised if there are slight differences between Irish and Scottish martens because they are genetically distinct – they are assigned to different haplotypes – and because the two populations have been isolated by the Irish Sea for a few thousand years.

We can speculate about the reasons why pine martens wear such striking bibs: it could be an example of 'countershading', which is believed to help conceal animals from predators by reducing shadow on their undersides in well-lit environments; but if this is the reason why do martens opt for a 'chest only' pale patch when stoats and weasels – arguably more vulnerable to predators because they are much smaller – go the whole hog with white or cream along their whole undersides? Or could it be an example of disruptive colouration, in which large blocks of highly contrasting colour with sharp boundaries prevent recognition of an animal's outline by another animal? Although in many cases disruptive colouration is used by prey species to evade their predators, in this case it might help a pine marten if it prevents a startled vole, for example, from identifying the marten-like shape looming over it. Or perhaps the bib has a role in communication or display between pine martens, like a badge or a flag to be waved when animals stand up to face each other; could it make a standing marten look more daunting in a territorial dispute or in an argument at a feeding station; or is bib colour linked to fitness in some way, so that boys with rich, apricot-coloured bibs are more attractive to the girls than those with paler bibs?

Until recently, I had not heard of unusual colour varieties of pine martens such as melanism, albinism or erythrism. However, thanks to Claire Poirson, I was alerted to a series of photographs on Facebook of what appears to be an albino or leucistic pine marten climbing a dead tree in the Lorraine region of north-eastern France (albinism involves a lack of the pigment melanin; leucism involves a more complete lack of pigmentation). The photographs were taken in October 2016 and posted on a Facebook page called *Au détour des sentiers* (roughly 'Off the beaten tracks'). The animal, clearly a marten, is entirely covered in yellowish-white fur, with a pale pink rhinarium and pink skin visible inside the ears. One cannot see whether the eyes are red, but the lack of dark pigmentation in the rhinarium and ears, and the yellowish-white fur colour, perhaps suggests that the animal is a true albino. Albinism is a genetically recessive fur colour that is likely to be very rare in pine martens because of its associated disadvantages of extreme visibility – except during snowy periods – to both predators and prey.

HORRENDOUS HISTORY

Downhill from a Mesolithic heyday
The pine marten had its heyday in Britain and Ireland when post-glacial tree cover was at its maximum in the Mesolithic, before our Neolithic ancestors started clearing the wildwood for agriculture some 6,000 years ago. Assuming near-continuous woodland cover and basing their calculations on modern pine marten abundance in Białowieża Forest – our closest surviving approximation to the wildwood in Europe today – Maroo and Yalden estimated that there were 147,474 pine martens in Britain during the Mesolithic. This figure indicates that the pine marten was then more abundant in Britain than any other carnivore except the weasel. Even then, the occurrence of fossil marten remains alongside human bones and artefacts at Mesolithic cave sites indicates that early humans had already started killing pine martens, probably for their fur.

From the Neolithic onwards, in both Ireland and Britain, humans caused a prolonged decline in pine marten abundance and distribution through progressive woodland clearance, trapping of martens for their valuable fur, general persecution of nuisance predators and, finally, ruthless predator eradication connected with game shooting. There is even a reference to an exotic dish known as 'marten's pottage' suggesting human consumption. Thanks to this combined onslaught, the pine marten is now scarcer than all other native carnivores (except the extinct ones) on our islands apart from the Scottish wildcat.

The confusing pattern of the pine marten's decline in Britain and Ireland
If my suspicion that the stone marten was once a resident of these islands is true, then its fading historical presence alongside the pine marten – combined with difficulty in distinguishing confidently between the two species – must have affected our ancestors' perceptions and our modern understanding of the pine marten's decline. This situation surely worsened following Alston's 1879 dictat, in which he asserted that all martens previously referred to in Britain can only have been pine martens. Consequently, any differences in the pattern of decline of the two species would have become (con)fused with – thanks to Alston – our later attempts to reconstruct the pattern of the pine marten's decline inevitably

based upon a messy and misleading merger of information from the two species.

A likely scenario is that through most of our historical times the stone or beech marten (also called the common marten, because that is how it was once perceived here) was the more abundant and widespread of the two in Britain, especially in the south, before effective predator removal began to eradicate both species from the 1700s onwards. However, thanks to its tendency to occupy human-modified environments and to use dens in or near human habitations, the stone marten was latterly eliminated more swiftly and more completely than the shy and retiring pine marten, which was typically described by naturalists writing in the eighteenth and nineteenth centuries as less common and 'of a wild disposition, keeps at a distance from human habitation, and resides in the least frequented forests and the thickest woods'. This idea clearly needs to be investigated further but, if it has any merit, it would go some way to explain why (again thanks to Alston) pine martens are now perhaps mistakenly perceived as having survived in the mainly deforested south of Britain for much longer than we might expect given their preference for well-wooded landscapes.

Pine martens killed as vermin

The pine marten belongs to the unfortunate band of wild mammals and birds classed as 'vermin' in former times, when it was generally deemed desirable to kill them whenever and wherever possible. This onslaught was encouraged by financial incentives such as the Irish law dating from 1787 under which five shillings was paid to anyone who destroyed a marten, with similar arrangements in Britain from 1532 onwards under the Tudor Vermin Acts. In his book *Silent Fields*, Roger Lovegrove explores the records of church wardens' bounty payments in the parishes of England and Wales. He notes that, compared with other carnivores such as the polecat and fox, rather few pine martens are reported as killed in most parishes. This may be due to their advancing rarity through the sixteenth and seventeenth centuries due to woodland clearance and over-exploitation for fur, and also perhaps because trappers could get a better price for a dead marten from a furrier than from a church warden.

In terms of the nuisance value that justified their killing in historical times, pine martens were mainly viewed as a threat to poultry; but there were occasional reports of them attacking sheep, which seems extraordinary considering the size difference between the two animals. In his 1892 *Vertebrate Fauna of Lakeland,* Macpherson reports that 'Shepherds sometimes complain of individual Martens worrying sheep, but it rarely happens that any such loss is inflicted upon farmers, whose worst enemies are the Foxes'. Pine martens were also cursed for raiding beehives for their honey, and for stealing plums, gooseberries and strawberries; in his 2001 book *A Basket of Weasels,* James Fairley describes several accounts of pine martens in Ireland getting into trouble because of their fondness for sweet food.

As for how pine martens were caught and killed in those early days before guns were widely available, it seems likely that they were caught in steel spring traps – precursors of the 'gin trap' – that held the animal by a leg until the trapper came to clobber the captive to death. Dead-fall traps were also used, in which bait was placed beneath a propped-up slab of rock that crushed the marten when it dislodged the stick supporting it. Martens were sometimes killed at their dens in hollow trees – often located by following their tracks in snow – where the occupant was smoked out and caught in a bag as it bolted. Live martens caught in this way apparently had even greater value than dead ones sold for their fur: writing in his *Vertebrate Fauna of Lakeland*, Macpherson reports that a live marten could sell for ten shillings to be baited by dogs in the West Cumbrian towns of Workington and Whitehaven.

Trapping for fur

Our ancestors' early appreciation of pine martens had everything to do with catching and killing them to remove their pelts. Such was the value of their fur that pine martens (as well as their close relatives the American marten and sable) were an important target for early fur-trappers across the northern hemisphere. They were part of the fur trade that kick-started commercial activity in Russia and fuelled European exploration across the colder parts of North America and Canada, where the export of pelts was so lucrative that they became known as 'soft gold'.

In *Silent Fields,* Lovegrove reports from various sources on the exploitation of pine martens for their fur in Britain, which began in Scotland as early as the fourteenth century. Inverness was the main centre for the trade in mertrick (marten) pelts, where the cold Highland winters ensured that Scottish marten pelts were of a higher quality than those from further south in Britain. Across Scotland large numbers of martens were trapped and killed for their fur between the fourteenth and nineteenth centuries, and many marten pelts were exported to other countries via Leith, with a customs levy of sixpence per 30 skins imposed in 1424.

Even in Gloucestershire one would be paid two shillings and sixpence (12.5 pence in modern currency) for a marten skin in 1829; and by 1892 MacPherson reported the price for a dog mart pelt was six shillings and sixpence (bitch pelts were a shilling less). In Ireland too, pine martens were trapped and sold for their fur in many places, with Lord Kenmare's gamekeeper reportedly earning seven shillings and sixpence for each marten he killed in 1877 in the Killarney area of County Kerry. According to Paddy O'Sullivan, who undertook the first ever pine marten survey of Ireland in the late 1970s, generations of rural people trapped and killed martens to sell their fur, only giving up in the 1950s because the animal became so scarce.

The pine marten's highly prized fur is likely to have led our ancestors to move live specimens to new places in order to guarantee a future supply of soft, warm clothing. For example, we know that pine martens were recorded living wild on the Outer Hebrides from 1549 until their extinction in the late 1800s. But naturalist Stewart Angus speculates that, because pine martens would surely struggle to swim across the fierce seas of the Minch, it is likely that they were deliberately introduced by humans at an early stage of their occupation of the islands.

It is also possible that the wild pine martens in Ireland today were originally transported across the water by early human settlers from Wales or England to provide a source of free-range fur coats. Research by James Fairley indicates that marten pelts were exported from Ireland to the UK from as early as 1430.

Hunting with hounds
Because of the pine marten's unsportsmanlike habit of climbing up a tree to safety when danger threatens, our hound-oriented sporting ancestors tended to concentrate on less arboreal quarry such as deer, hares, foxes

and otters. However, in those places where trees were absent so the martens had to play fair, such as on the bare, rocky fell-sides of northern England, hunting with hounds was more feasible – though due to the tricky terrain the human participants had to follow on foot rather than on horseback. Several packs were dedicated to 'hunting the mart', which was especially associated with the rugged fells and dales of the Lake District, but also occurred in the Welsh mountains. In contrast, there are rather few references to this form of sport in Ireland, although Arthur Stringer wrote extensively about his experience of hunting marterns, as he called them, on the Portmore Estate beside Lough Neagh.

In his *Vertebrate Fauna of Lakeland*, Macpherson reproduces Mr W. A. Durnford's 'picturesque' account of a marten hunt starting in Wastdale (now called Wasdale), first published in *The Field* in 1879. It describes the human followers' rigorous climb of Yewbarrow (a 2,000+ foot mountain) with six couple of hounds 'varying in size from a beagle to a foxhound, with three wire-haired terriers':

Once the hounds picked up the fresh scent of a 'mart' among the crags, they were 'clambering up with an agility which would astonish their relations further south, resembling a party of squirrels rather than members of the canine race, as they vie with one another in their anxiety to be to the fore'.

After an hour the marten took refuge deep in a rock crevice from which, because the terriers could not bolt it, the animal was smoked out: 'We all set to work to gather as much grass as the locality afforded; the huntsman produced from his capacious pockets a box of matches, a little gunpowder, and an old newspaper, and in a few minutes a fire which consisted of smoke rather than flame was burning as far down the crevice as the fuel could be thrust….. in less than three minutes a long dark object was seen scampering above our heads, having escaped out of a hole a little distance off.

Away we went again, both hounds and men more excited than ever, leaping from crag to crag, and performing acrobatic feats from which any one would have shrunk in cold blood.' After taking refuge in some boulders the 'mart' was bolted by the terriers – 'bravely the little creature raced on' – until a mile further on it was killed by the hounds on open ground as it headed towards Pillar Mountain.

Macpherson explains that such marten hunts traditionally took place only in winter (although in 1877 Durnford reportedly wrote that marten hunting took place in all seasons in Cumberland, Westmorland and Lancashire) and the success rate was rather low, probably because the quarry so often found a rocky crevice from which it could be flushed neither by terriers nor smoke. Through his many contacts in Lakeland, Macpherson concluded that, even when martens were common, it was unusual for as many as five or six to be killed in a single winter in any one of Eskdale, Wastdale, Martindale and Patterdale. Nevertheless, even this number could have made a considerable dent in the local population.

Game shooting

Starting in Britain with the Game Laws of 1671, the rise of game shooting as a recreation for the wealthy classes marked the start of a new and devastatingly effective phase in the eradication of carnivores and birds of prey. As predators of game, pine martens were trapped, shot and poisoned by the growing army of gamekeepers that were employed in Britain and Ireland to ensure that there were enough pheasants, partridges and grouse for the guns to shoot. This pressure was probably less widespread and less intensive in Ireland than across the water in Britain, simply because there were fewer traditional sporting estates so the abundance of gamekeepers was much lower there: in 1851 there were reportedly 591 gamekeepers in the whole of Ireland; in 1870 in England and Wales there were more than 12,000.

In his 1992 book *Game Heritage*, Stephen Tapper describes the development of the game-keeping profession through the eighteenth and nineteenth centuries, culminating in the early 1900s when more than 23,000 gamekeepers were working in Britain. In pursuit of the primary aim of producing and maintaining an unnaturally large surplus of game for the guns to shoot, one of the gamekeeper's main tasks was to eradicate all predators on his patch. Tapper observes that at that time 'Most of Britain was covered with a contiguous network of well keepered estates, so that virtually every corner of the countryside was subject to this continuous destruction of vermin on a scale that is almost unbelievable today'. Good shooting estates typically employed about 2.5 gamekeepers for every 1,000 hectares and deployed a high density of steel traps set in field boundaries and around woodlands, which would have been especially effective at catching all the smaller mustelids, including pine martens.

Initially constrained neither by protected species legislation (pine martens did not receive full legal protection until 1976 in Ireland and 1988 in Britain) nor by wider societal concerns about suffering by animals held in steel traps or snares, or killed by poison, gamekeepers were free to deploy a variety of methods to eliminate predators. Some insight into the numbers killed can be gained from the records kept by shooting estates at the time. For example, at Glengarry in Inverness-shire (where pine martens are common again today), more 'Marten Cats' were killed over a three-year period than any other single carnivore (stoats and weasels were lumped together; see table below). For a slow-breeding species like the pine marten this widespread and sustained pressure was too great for the population to bear, so a wide-scale decline in range and abundance was inevitable; in contrast, the more densely packed populations of faster-breeding stoats and weasels were better equipped to replace the huge numbers killed by gamekeepers, so managed to remain widely established in Britain.

'Vermin' species	Numbers killed 1837–1840
Foxes	11
Wild Cats	198
Marten Cats	246
Polecats	106
Stoats and Weasels	301
Badgers	67
Otters	48
House Cats	78

Vermin mammals killed over a three-year period on a sporting estate in Glengarry, Inverness-shire (extracted from Grouse and Grouse Moors by George Malcolm, first published in 1910).

Habitat loss

Woodland clearance, started by Neolithic farmers across Europe as a precursor to settled agriculture, was very bad news for the pine marten.

Britain and Ireland were deforested earlier and more completely than most other countries in the pine marten's range: according to Oliver Rackham 'half of England had ceased to be wildwood by 500 BC'; by Domesday (1086) woodland cover over most of England had fallen to 15 per cent, and was below 10 per cent in parts of the south and east; and thereafter woods were destroyed at an average rate of at least 20 acres a day.

Although woodland clearance was less well documented in Ireland, Scotland and Wales, it is likely to have followed a similar pattern. By 1895, woodland cover in Britain had fallen to just below 5 per cent – and below 2 per cent in counties like Cambridgeshire – with most surviving woodlands much less than 100 hectares in size. Pine martens would still have been instinctively drawn to these woods, yet most were a focus for activities such as cutting of firewood and timber, hunting with hounds and gamekeeping. So, one can imagine how challenging conditions were for pine martens as the nadir of woodland cover approached at the end of the nineteenth century: more than 90 per cent of their preferred habitat had been removed; most of the remaining fragments were too small and scattered across open farmland to support a single pine marten home range; and woodlands were typically worked by a rural human population quick to kill any martens they encountered.

Differences between Britain and Ireland

The pine marten's decline in Ireland occurred later than it did in Britain, probably because of the lower intensity of game-keeping pressures reported above. Although woodland clearance, general persecution and trapping for fur and in connection with game rearing had a substantial impact on the local abundance of pine martens in Ireland, the species remained relatively widespread into the twentieth century. The intensification of sheep-farming in the 1950s and the associated use of the poison strychnine to control predators was, according to Paddy O'Sullivan, the critical factor that tipped the balance and led to the disappearance of pine martens from many areas in the 1950s and 60s. A hundred years earlier, pine martens were already absent from huge areas of Britain; by 1915, thanks to the efficient predator eradication by gamekeepers, the species was mainly confined to north-west Scotland and small pockets in northern England and North Wales.

WHERE DID MARTENS SURVIVE AND WHY?

At their respective nadirs in Britain and Ireland pine martens survived best where humans – and especially gamekeepers – were scarcest and where the landscape offered alternative habitats to their preferred woodland, which was extremely scarce at the end of the nineteenth century. Pine martens took refuge in the rugged, wet and windy western fringes of our islands, where rocky mountainsides, crags, scree slopes and boulder fields provided vertical habitat features similar to those found in woodland.

In their 1977 paper on 'The decline of the rarer carnivores in Great Britain during the nineteenth century', Langley and Yalden identified three main areas where pine martens survived at their nadir in 1915. The largest of these was in the rugged north-west Highlands of Scotland centred on western Sutherland, western Ross and Cromarty, Lochaber and Inverness. Next largest were the fells of Lakeland in the north-west of England; and the last and smallest was centred on the mountains of Snowdonia in North Wales. It is no coincidence that these three areas represent the rockiest places in the whole of Britain, based upon their unusual concentration of rocky features identifiable on Ordnance Survey maps. Some pine martens apparently survived in other places, such as the Pennines and the mountains of southern Wales.

Based on modern home-range data gathered by David Balharry during his radio-tracking in the north-west of Scotland, we can derive estimates of the number of pine martens in each of these refugia in 1915: at 15,000 square kilometres the north-west Scotland refugium supported roughly 1,500 pine martens; Lakeland supported 400 and Snowdonia just 100. So, the British total population had fallen from an estimated Mesolithic maximum of 147,474 to a pitiful 2,000 in the early 1900s – a numerical decline of more than 98 per cent.

Although Frank Fraser Darling, in respect of the population in the treeless mountains of north-west Scotland, described this shift to rocky uplands as an 'extraordinary adaptation to another way of life', the martens were simply selecting the next-best available habitat in the absence of their preferred woodland. Indeed, their apparent selection of the rockiest places, rather than the areas with the lowest density of gamekeepers, suggests that the pine martens' distribution at the time of lowest woodland cover was determined as much by active habitat selection as by a retreat from human culling pressures.

When woodland cover was at its lowest, pine martens adapted their superb climbing skills to survive among cliffs, crags and rocky mountains in the north and west of Britain and Ireland.

In Ireland, there was a similar retreat to the rocky west: by the time of Paddy O'Sullivan's distribution survey in the late 1970s the species was mainly confined to the west coast counties between and including Limerick in the south and Sligo in the north, with Galway and Clare being particular strongholds – notably pine martens survived in The Burren in County Clare, where craggy limestone pavement and hazel woodlands provided a refuge (and where I saw my first Irish pine marten); and there were smaller outlier populations probably surviving in the counties of Louth, Waterford, Cork and Kerry.

SURVIVAL AND SLOW, PARTIAL RECOVERY

For pine martens and other beleaguered predators, the First World War (1914–1918) was a crucial turning point in Britain and Ireland: culling was substantially reduced while game shooting was put on hold during the war years, with many gamekeepers leaving the land to fight for the allies in Europe. After the war, there was not the same intensity of predator eradication and the Second World War of 1939–1945 had a similar effect, so by 1951 the number of gamekeepers in Britain had fallen to 4,391. In parts of the Highlands of Scotland there were even the tentative beginnings of a conservation movement among enlightened landowners who realised how close to extinction the pine marten had been driven – in the 1920s and '30s Colonel E. J. Fergusson implored estates to stop killing the martens and some acted on his advice. Nevertheless, signs of recovery were very slow to emerge, and it wasn't until 1939 that there were reports of pine martens expanding their range in north-west Scotland.

I suggest three things combined to prevent pine martens from bouncing back swiftly once culling pressure eased in the second decade of the twentieth century: firstly, their naturally low reproductive rate limited the capacity of populations to increase quickly once conditions improved; secondly, their rugged, tree-less refugia were characterised by unproductive habitats in which prey biomass and diversity were low, so pine marten populations existed at low densities and were further constrained by lower than average kit productivity; and finally, although there were fewer gamekeepers, culling had not stopped entirely, so pine martens were still killed deliberately and as incidental victims of the expansion in rabbit-trapping in the 1940s and early 1950s (the pre-myxomatosis boom in rabbit populations was one consequence of the earlier eradication of so many predators).

In Ireland, pine marten recovery involved a post-1970s eastward expansion from the main western refuge into the midlands of the Republic. The main reasons for this recovery are believed to be the near-doubling in the area of forestry since the 1980s, with reduced persecution following legal protection for pine martens in the Republic under the Wildlife Act

(1976). Further expansion in the south-west arose as a consequence of a reintroduction to Killarney National Park; this involved translocation of up to 30 martens from the west of Ireland during the late 1980s and early 1990s; further isolated populations may have arisen as a result of unrecorded translocations where pine martens were relocated from areas where they were in conflict with human activities. In Northern Ireland, by the 2000s there was little evidence of expansion of the small population in the far west, giving cause for concern about its future.

Pine martens did eventually recover in Scotland, with a slow repopulation across the Highlands tracked through the late twentieth century and into the new millennium by distribution surveys in the early 1980s, the mid-1990s and the mid-2010s. Recolonisation of the intensive game-shooting area of north-east Scotland was especially slow, leading the authors of the mid-1990s survey to hint that the impact of predator control on pine martens should be closely scrutinised if things didn't improve. Elsewhere, by the end of the twentieth century, pine martens had begun to spread beyond the rugged Highlands into busier lowland landscapes, providing opportunities for people to get to know the animal once again. This process was assisted by the first publicised translocation of pine martens – from the Highlands to Galloway Forest by the Forestry Commission in the early 1980s – leading to the establishment of a new population in south-west Scotland. Though tainted and constrained by continuing illegal persecution, this recovery of an iconic Scottish mammal was something to celebrate against the prevailing trend of biodiversity loss. But things were rather different south of the Scottish border.

In a few parts of southern Britain pine martens survived in special rocky places long enough into the twentieth century for encounters to be recalled within living memory. I am indebted to my friend Huw Denman for sharing his translation of an interview with his father, aged 87 at the time, conducted in Welsh in their native Carmarthenshire in early 2016. Old Mr Denman worked for the Forestry Commission in various parts of Wales from the early 1950s, and recalls two encounters with pine martens. The first was in about 1953 near Dolgellau, where a local trapper took home a young pine marten after killing its mother high on the crags of Rhobell (a craggy mountain east of Coed y Brenin Forest). The trapper's daughter tamed and raised the young marten, and Mr Denman recalls visiting their house where he saw it sitting on her lap. Later, one night in the 1970s, he saw a wild one as he drove home through Llanllawddog: a long dark animal ran across the road and shot up a tree; its long tail was clearly visible so there was no doubt it was a pine marten; and others were seeing them at the same time in and around Brechfa Forest in Carmarthenshire.

The 'mythical' martens of England and Wales

Nobody sensible disputes the evidence, collated by Langley and Yalden, that in the early 1900s pine martens remained in parts of northern England and North Wales. However, one of the great British wildlife enigmas was whether they were still there towards the end of that century, and the evidence was hotly debated. From the 1950s onwards a handful of naturalists had doggedly recorded the elusive presence of pine martens persisting in a few core areas. Against a background of increasing scepticism from the establishment, their efforts and commitment were remarkable.

The extensive poetry and prose of Colin Simms records his tireless fieldwork since 1955 among the fells of northern England. He recorded pine martens from the Cheviots and north Pennines down to suburban South and West Yorkshire, and from the Lakeland fells across to the Cleveland coast. Notably Simms also detected the presence of American martens – probably escapees from fur farms – in Northumberland, something later confirmed by geneticists who revealed evidence of their hybridisation with pine martens. In North Wales, Duncan Brown logged sightings of pine martens from the 1980s that showed they still survived in their Snowdonia stronghold; Ian Morgan collated records that confirmed martens had also survived long-term into the same decade in a southern Welsh stronghold centred on Carmarthenshire and Brecknock; and Andrew Lucas later concluded they were still present in Carmarthenshire into the 1990s.

A frustrating feature of these sparse marten populations in England and Wales was the scarcity of detectable field signs, which encouraged doubters that no viable populations remained. Soon after Paddy O'Sullivan's late 1970s survey in Ireland, Kathy Velander undertook the first national pine marten field survey of Britain for the VWT in 1980–1982: she had no trouble finding marten scats on her 1-kilometre transects in Scotland; but none of the known strongholds further south revealed such evidence; nevertheless, her interviews with local naturalists led her to believe that martens were still present in England and Wales but faring less well than the main Scottish population, for which Velander had reported further range expansion in the Highlands.

Velander's findings prompted a new pine marten survey in the late 1980s (not published by the Joint Nature Conservation Committee until 1996), which focused on five core areas of England and Wales: Population A in Northumberland/eastern Cumbria and Durham; Population B in North Yorkshire; Population C in Cumbria/Lancashire; Population D in West and South Yorkshire/Derbyshire; and Population E in Wales. With fieldwork by the late Rob Strachan (based on 2-kilometre scat transects to increase the chances of detection) and collation of 861 post-1800 records by Don Jefferies, the results rang loud alarm bells: while all populations were believed to be extant in 1988, they seemed to exist at vanishingly low population densities and most were contracting (Populations B, C and D) or static (E); only Population A might have been spreading; and we have to bear in mind that scat identification during this survey was in the less rigorous era prior to genetic verification. A further revelation from this survey was that the 'certainty' of pine marten records declined during the twentieth century: for example, there was a shift from records being dominated by bodies of martens killed during predator control to those involving live sightings or field signs; this was felt to be partly a consequence of the greater scarcity of martens and the reluctance of people to admit to killing them, even though full legal protection wasn't afforded to the species until 1988 in Britain.

John Messenger and I joined the quest while working for the VWT in the 1990s, and set about developing a more rigorous way of evaluating the sightings still being reported. We designed a questionnaire to ensure we asked the right questions in the right way, and biostatistician Simon Poulton designed MARTRECS, a database still used by the VWT to store and analyse records of pine martens from England and Wales. Between 1996 and 2007 we received 524 reports – mostly live sightings – that we believed were probably of pine martens. Where a sighting was both reliable and fresh we sometimes searched the location for field signs, with remarkably little success (aptly described by Durham naturalist Terry Coult as 'looking for things that aren't there').

Despite the years that have passed, I can still recall many conversations that left me in no doubt that the interviewee had encountered a pine marten: there was the 2004 sighting of an animal up a tree in Consall Wood Nature Reserve (backed up by a good photograph) in Staffordshire; in 1996 Chris Hall saw one cross a ravine at dusk at Plas Tan-y-Bwlch in Merioneth; in 2002 Toby Fisher saw a pine marten run up a tree at Claife Heights in Cumbria; in 2001 an off-duty police officer reported a marten running up a tree in Kidland Forest in Northumberland; in 1999 a pine marten was flushed by sheepdogs on the edge of Crychan Forest in Powys, where it ran up a tree and was observed for over a minute by a group of farmers moving their sheep; and I have to mention the famous 'Critchley skull' – the remains of a pine marten killed in a fox snare and recovered by forester Charles Critchley from a gamekeeper's midden near Broughton Bank on the North York Moors in 1993 (the skull is now preserved in The National Museums of Scotland in Edinburgh).

Our analysis of the MARTRECS data suggested that pine martens were still present, though rare, in the same core areas in which they had been recorded in previous decades: our records were concentrated in Snowdonia and Carmarthenshire in Wales, and in Lakeland, Northumbria and the North Yorkshire Moors in England. However, the genetic evidence already presented above indicates that the original relict haplotype *i* had probably been lost earlier in the century, so the animals we recorded were most likely descendents of escapees or animals covertly translocated from Scotland; and they were clearly struggling, with no signs of population recovery to lift our flagging spirits.

Why didn't the 'southern' pine marten populations recover in the manner of those in Scotland? With their smaller populations, had they dropped below some critical numerical threshold that made decline towards functional extinction inevitable? Or was there a fundamental environmental change that had a more harmful impact upon pine martens in England and Wales compared with Scotland? If I had to pick one likely culprit it would be the staggering post-1950 increase in sheep populations grazing the uplands of England and Wales – the very areas to which pine martens had retreated in the early 1900s. We know how overgrazing can damage upland habitats and erode biodiversity – George Monbiot's term 'Sheep-wrecked' seems apt – so this just might have tipped the balance for struggling marten populations in the late twentieth century.

CURRENT DISTRIBUTION AND STATUS

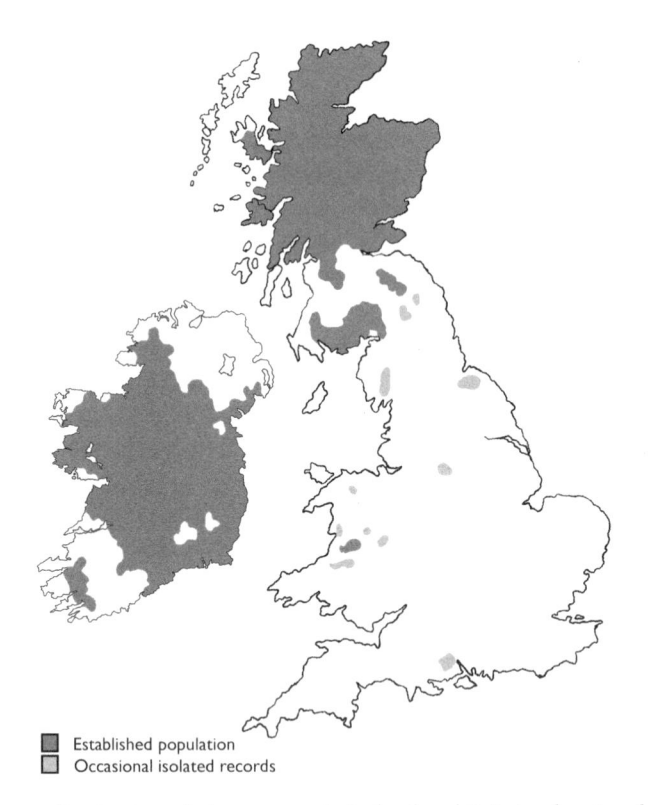

The current distribution of pine martens in Ireland and Britain, showing the areas supporting established populations and those with occasional records only.

Ireland

Scat surveys across the whole of Ireland organised by Declan O'Mahony during 2005–2007, with DNA confirmation by Catherine O'Reilly and Pete Turner, informed the most recent distribution map. This showed that in the Republic the pine marten had expanded its range since O'Sullivan's 1978–1980 survey identified the main refuge areas more than 25 years earlier: the range now occupies much of the west and midlands, with further isolated populations in the south-west, south-east and east; in Northern Ireland recolonisation is less advanced, with pine martens mainly found in the south-west of the jurisdiction.

Scotland

Scat-based distribution surveys in 2012 and 2013 (in which Dooley and I played a small part), led by Lizzie Croose of the VWT on behalf of Scottish Natural Heritage, give us the best indication of current pine marten distribution in Scotland. A hundred years since their nadir, pine martens have recolonised most of mainland Scotland to the north of the central lowland belt. Although there may still be a few marten-free places in the unforested far north and extreme east of the mainland, the species' recolonisation here is essentially complete. With human help, martens have recently appeared on two offshore islands and are in the process of colonising them: Skye (martens popped over from the mainland via the new bridge completed in 1995) and Mull (martens were probably translocated from the mainland accidentally or deliberately around 2004).

South of the central lowland belt, a long-established pine marten population is present in and around Galloway Forest following the 1980s reintroduction, and unofficial translocations since 2007 have re-established a population in the Upper Tweed Valley in Peebleshire. Natural dispersal across the River Clyde via the Erskine Bridge might explain the recent (2013) evidence of martens south-west of Glasgow in North Renfrewshire. Further south there is now evidence of pine martens in east Dumfriesshire, with recent records from close to the English border.

Wales

The very sparse Welsh populations of uncertain status have been reinforced since the VWT started translocating Scottish pine martens to mid-Wales in autumn 2015 (see *The VWT's Pine Marten Recovery Project*, page 179). A breeding population is now re-established in the forests cloaking the Cambrian Mountains east of Aberystwyth, and one can find marten scats along many forest tracks that confirm this exciting fact. This reinforced population is likely to expand slowly if conditions are suitable. Elsewhere in Wales, sightings of pine martens are still occasionally reported.

England

The VWT occasionally receives reliable reports of pine martens from the same core areas occupied at the turn of the millennium: Northumbria, the North York Moors, Lakeland and the South Pennines. Beyond these traditional patches, pine martens are also popping up in some surprising places.

The recent expansion in the use of camera traps has produced clear images or video clips that confirm the presence of wild pine martens. In March 2015 student Jack Merritt filmed a pine marten near Bude in North Cornwall; also in 2015, following a photograph taken by Dave Pearce in July of that year, Stuart Edmunds of Shropshire Wildlife Trust's Pine Marten Project deployed camera traps and secured more than 20 photographs and videos of wild pine martens in South Shropshire (by spring 2017 Stuart had gathered a further 35 camera images and videos that confirm the presence of at least eight pine martens, based on examination of their bib patterns); in March 2016 Russell Wynn and Marcus Ward obtained several photographs and video clips of a pine marten in the New Forest in Hampshire; in June 2016 a pine marten was photographed by Paul Birch in the abandoned village of Tyneham near the Purbeck Hills in Dorset; and in July 2017 'NatureSpy' recorded an adult male pine marten on Forestry Commission land in North Yorkshire.

It is fun to speculate about the origins of these pine martens recently detected in southern Britain well away from known strongholds: although it is very tempting to believe they may have lurked undetected for decades (just waiting for a camera trap to cavort in front of), it is more likely that they have escaped from captivity or simply been released after a long journey south from the Scottish Highlands (see section on covert releases, page 178); and the genetic evidence – if available – usually supports the latter scenario.

On a more positive note, pine martens are poised to recolonise northern England from new populations expanding in the Scottish Borders, with evidence of martens reported from Kielder Forest in 2016, and a Northumberland carcass recovered in 2017. Encouragingly, the VWT is working with Natural England to facilitate this natural recovery through a project known as *Back from the Brink*.

PHOTOGRAPHS BY TERRY WHITTAKER

An adult female pine marten in summer pelage on the Black Isle in Scotland stands up to get a better view, showing her striking yellow bib and strong dark-furred forelegs. The tufts of pale fur around the claws on the forefeet are characteristic of some older animals.

Top: A pine marten has detected prey from an elevated branch on the Black Isle, with the night sky tinted orange by the lights of Inverness.
Bottom: This pine marten – photographed in September – is showing its distinctive bib pattern, which can enable naturalists to identify individuals.

The pine marten leaps from the branch. Photographed in November, this animal is in its thick, medium-brown winter pelage.

Top: A pine marten in winter pelage moves along a high branch.
(The Black Isle, October)
Bottom: A pine marten descends a tree, showing how the rear feet can be rotated so as to grip the bark to allow a safe descent. Photographed in September, the animal's thick winter coat is beginning to grow.

This marten kit of 4–5 months old already has the alert, poised demeanor of an adult. (The Black Isle, July)

An Irish pine marten in summer pelage is attracted to a hair tube by the smell of fresh chicken bait. (County Waterford)

Above: As it forces its way up the tube to reach the bait at the top, the pine marten leaves a few hairs on the sticky patches inside the tube near the bottom.

Right: Fresh pine marten hairs on a sticky patch retrieved from a hair tube, containing sufficient DNA to reveal the genotype of the individual.

A male pine marten (note the visible testes) in summer pelage in County Waterford; compared with Scottish martens this one has the shorter, blotchier bib characteristic of Irish pine martens.

A pine marten in winter pelage raids a red squirrel feeder for peanuts. (The Black Isle, April)

A pine marten descends a tree carrying a bird's egg in its mouth. (The Black Isle, September)

Pine marten kits aged 4–5 months perfect their climbing skills; although nearly full-grown, they can be separated from more tatty-coated adults like the one opposite by their pristine fur. (The Black Isle, July)

This adult female pine marten has the slight 'scruffing' on the back of her neck that suggests she may have been mated recently. (The Black Isle, July)

Three young pine martens on the Black Isle in July; litters larger than this are unusual in Scotland.

An adult female marten carrying prey crosses a road. The short summer pelage shows the animal's slim, leggy shape. (The Black Isle; July)

An adult pine marten in full winter pelage; the large size and broad head of this animal suggest that it is a male. (The Black Isle, February)

This image of a leggy young pine marten 'following its nose' up a branch epitomises the busy energy and agility of the species. (The Black Isle, July)

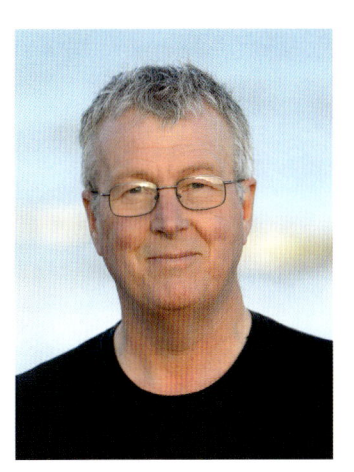

Terry Whittaker has been a freelance editorial photographer since 2000 following a career in zoos and wildlife conservation around the world. Specialising in the relationship between people and nature, commissions and personal projects include the water vole conservation, urban nature and wildlife habitat restoration in the UK.

He has been photographing pine martens, initially in Ireland and then Scotland, since 2008. He uses a variety of techniques including long lens photography from a small canvas hide in the forest and makes extensive use of DSLR camera traps where the marten triggers the camera when it breaks an invisible infrared beam.

More of Terry's images can be seen on his website: www.terrywhittaker.com

Pine marten scats photographed in Scotland by J. Birks and J. Martin, showing the diversity of colours and textures influenced by their varied contents; many have the distinctive loopy shape of scats produced with a 'hip-wiggle'.

MODERN MARTEN HABITATS

Woodland specialist or habitat generalist?
There are three essential components of pine marten habitat that enable a population to thrive: abundant and diverse sources of food to sustain foraging pine martens throughout the year; safe den sites for resting, sheltering from bad weather and for successful breeding; and levels of mortality that do not exceed the rather low reproductive output of the population. Whether consciously or otherwise, these three elements guide each young dispersing pine marten as it makes the crucial decision where to settle and establish a home range.

Pine martens, as their name suggests, have a strong association with trees and woodland. The 'pine' prefix is misleading, however, because pine martens are not fussy about whether they live in broadleaved or coniferous woodland so long as it provides sufficient food, safe resting sites and general security: the high tree canopy and cluttered understorey of mature woodland provides protection against larger birds of prey, such as golden eagles, which may kill pine martens as food; and trees offer above-ground escape routes from terrestrial predators such as foxes.

For many years, we have tended to view the pine marten as a habitat specialist that is heavily dependent upon extensive woodland. The conventional view has been that pine martens avoid open spaces and favour extensive 'old growth' (meaning ancient and unmanaged) woodland because it has the structural complexity and abundance of tree cavities to meet all their needs. However, this view has been challenged by recent studies in Scotland, France and Italy, which suggest that pine martens can make use of some non-wooded habitats, and that an element of woodland fragmentation may actually benefit them in some circumstances.

Fiona Caryl's radio-tracking study in Morangie Forest in northern Scotland showed that, although pine martens had a strong preference for mature woodland, they also favoured two open habitats within their home ranges: tussock grassland and scrub. Martens of both genders selected these open habitats, but Caryl found significant differences in the extent to which they travelled out of wooded areas to visit them: males typically travelled 75 metres away from woodland; whereas the females typically travelled just 30 metres from woodland. Also, males were located outside wooded habitats more frequently (46 per cent of male radio locations) than were females (33 per cent of female radio locations). These gender differences may be a consequence of the smaller size of the female martens, making them more vulnerable to certain 'open space' predators such as foxes and birds of prey; or they could be linked to their maternal duties and associated risk-averse behaviour leading them to stay closer to the protective cover of woodland for the sake of their dependent young.

Caryl's discovery of martens favouring certain open habitats in and around Morangie Forest led her to compare her findings with those of five other Scottish pine marten field studies in which, as at Morangie, home range sizes had been determined by radio-tracking and where dietary information was also available from scat analysis. The study sites had varying degrees of woodland fragmentation, with proportions of woodland cover that ranged from as low as 4 per cent in David Balharry's late 1980s study at Kinlochewe in north-west Scotland to 47 per cent in Paul Bright and Terry Smithson's 1990s study in Galloway Forest in south-west Scotland. Across the six studies Caryl found a strong positive correlation between the extent of woodland fragmentation and the abundance of small rodents – principally the field vole – in the pine martens' diets so that, as wooded landscapes became more fragmented, small rodents constituted a greater proportion of the martens' diet. The crucial factor in this relationship (in view of the martens' reluctance to stray too far from woodland) was believed to be the length of woodland edge in the landscape that, in turn, influenced the martens' access to small rodent habitats such as tussock grassland.

Caryl also found a relationship between pine marten home range size and woodland fragmentation, although it was not a simple, linear one: home ranges were smallest at intermediate levels of woodland fragmentation, where the extent of woodland cover lay between 25 and 30 per cent; and home ranges were larger at both extremes of the fragmentation scale. Since home range size reflects habitat quality and is a key determinant of population density it follows that, in Scotland at least, moderately fragmented wooded landscapes represent better habitat than more extensive woodland because they support more pine martens. A separate study in France, using a different approach, reached pretty much the same conclusion, as we shall see below.

In the Ardennes in north-eastern France Marina Mergey and colleagues extracted DNA from scats to estimate pine marten abundance in two contrasting areas: one dominated by dense forest; and one comprising smaller woodlands (amounting to 20 per cent woodland cover) scattered across an open agricultural landscape with abundant hedgerows and tree lines. Surprisingly, pine martens were more abundant in the farmed landscape with scattered woodlands, with a density of 8.5 martens per 10 square kilometres, compared with 6.1 martens per 10 square kilometres in the dense woodland. However, it may be relevant that hedgerows in France tend to be tall and tree-lined when compared with our typically flailed and stunted hedges in much of Britain, and this characteristic may provide important arboreal connectivity between French woodlands for martens that cannot be relied upon on our islands. However, some places have retained good densities of old hedgerow trees within the agricultural landscape, such as in parts of rural Ireland and Carmarthenshire in Wales, where martens may find it easier to commute safely between woodlands than they would in the intensive arable prairies of eastern England, for example.

An earlier radio-tracking study in the same Ardennes study area by Vincent Pereboom, Marina Mergey and colleagues had shown how pine martens moved through a landscape characterised by woodland fragments scattered over open farmland. When moving across fields they stayed closer to woodland cover than would be expected if their movements had been random; and on average martens remained within 42 metres of woodland edges or lines of trees, presumably to minimise the risk of predation in open areas. Although the French study found no gender difference in this woodland-hugging behaviour, the figure of 42 metres is in the same ballpark as the 30 and 75 metres found for females and males by Caryl in her Morangie study. So, this reluctance to stray too far from woodland would be a significant constraint upon pine marten occupancy and movements in landscapes where woodland cover is very low and highly fragmented, such as across much of the more intensive farmland of Britain and Ireland. However, a study in north-west Italy by Alessandro Balestrieri and colleagues – albeit based on DNA-typed scats and road-killed martens rather than radio-tracking – suggests that pine martens have recently expanded their range into the agricultural landscapes of the Western River Po Plain where woodland cover is very limited.

Finally, a wider analysis of pine marten habitat use in Highland Scotland was based on camera trapping from 2010 to 2013 at 27 sites across an area of some 50,000 square kilometres. Although the study focussed on wildcats as part of Kerry Kilshaw's PhD research, so many photographs of pine martens were recorded as 'by-catch' that Remington Moll led an exercise to mine the data for information on their broad-scale habitat use. Using an occupancy model approach (scientist-speak for cunning prediction), Moll and colleagues found that although pine martens were associated with wooded habitats in Scotland, they also occupied a variety of other habitats such as the vicinity of man-made structures (e.g. buildings), heather moorland, semi-natural grassland and even some agricultural land. In considering their findings, Moll and co. comment that the absence of stone martens – a key competitor on the European continent – might enable pine martens in Scotland to adopt a less woodland-focussed approach to habitat use (and the same would apply in Ireland too).

Considering the reasons why pine martens in Scotland might favour some open habitats alongside their general preference for woodland cover, Caryl noted that modern, managed woodlands – and especially the structurally simple conifer plantations established in the twentieth century – lack many of the characteristics associated with 'old growth' woodland, such as huge old trees, multi-layered woodland canopies, dense understorey thickets, and abundant standing and fallen deadwood. Where such features are scarce or absent pine martens may find it harder to avoid predators, forage efficiently and find elevated and insulated den sites. Caryl speculates that, as a consequence, martens choose to exploit alternative non-wooded habitats in order to access the missing resources. An alternative suggestion is that, thanks to the activities of large herbivores, primeval lowland European landscapes comprised a mosaic of wooded and open habitats (note that this 'wood pasture' hypothesis is contested by a namesake of mine, H. J. B. Birks, who argues that the evidence supports a hypothesis of extensive primeval closed canopy high forest), so perhaps pine martens today are simply continuing an ancient pattern of habitat use.

To illustrate her point Caryl refers to denning behaviour by the smaller female martens, which are more vulnerable to predation and incur greater energetic costs than do the larger males. Areas of dense ground cover provide important resting sites for martens (especially where elevated tree cavities are absent), and the females in Caryl's study showed a strong avoidance of areas where such ground cover was lacking, including closed canopy conifer woodland where heavy shading and browsing by deer reduces ground cover to zero (this also removes cover for small rodent populations so there is less food for martens to eat). Instead the female martens selected areas of scrub and tussock grassland, partly because of the safe resting sites they provided and, especially in the case of tussock grassland, for the populations of small rodents such as field voles that they supported. This was memorably illustrated when I visited Fiona Caryl during her Morangie Forest field study in September 2006 and we located a radio-tagged female marten resting under thick gorse and broome scrub on a grassy ride in the forest. Despite about six of us surrounding the patch of scrub, the radio signal revealed that the marten slipped away from her resting site without any of us seeing her.

One caveat we should bear in mind when considering the use of open, non-wooded habitats by pine martens is the 'fox factor'. Through the threat they pose as an important predator, foxes are very likely to influence patterns of pine marten habitat use: what may be safe in Scotland, where foxes are less abundant, may be suicidal in southern Britain where foxes are very common in the large open spaces between the small and scattered woodlands. So, where foxes are abundant, we should expect pine martens to be much more cautious about the extent to which they use open habitats. Furthermore, if Fiona Carly's hypothesis is correct, this may prevent martens from accessing some of the resources they need, which may in turn limit the success of populations in areas of open 'foxy' countryside.

Going underground in Nietoperek, Poland
Being an inquisitive and opportunistic carnivore, the pine marten sometimes finds valuable sources of food in unusual places. During the course of annual winter counts of hibernating bats in the subterranean Nietoperek tunnels (part of the Międzyrzecz Fortified Front constructed

by Hitler's army during the 1930s and now disused) in Western Poland, the VWT's Henry Schofield and Tomasz Kokurewicz of Wrocław University noticed accumulations of marten scats deep inside the tunnel system. Many of the scats were found to contain the remains of bats, so it seemed that one or more martens had discovered the tempting concentrations of up to 40,000 bats of ten species hibernating in the tunnels each winter. Although both stone and pine martens occur in that part of central Europe, Henry and Tomasz assumed that the culprit was the stone marten – and I agreed – because exploring underground tunnels in total darkness was more typical of that species than the pine marten, which tends to concentrate on climbing trees. How wrong we were!

Collection of marten scats from throughout the Nietoperek tunnel system between 2011 and 2014 produced the raw material for a ground-breaking PhD study by John Power. He was based at Catherine O'Reilly's 'Gene-genie' lab in Waterford, with the study receiving crucial support from Pete Turner, the VWT and their Polish friends, and including volunteers like me from many countries. This effort concentrated on collecting and recording the precise location of 1785 scats, including 659 scats from above-ground locations in case these revealed extra information about the martens using the tunnel system.

Despite the technical challenge of extracting high-quality DNA from marten scats that had been lurking for weeks in the humid subterranean tunnels, John Power's analyses confirmed that both pine and stone martens made extensive use of the tunnel system, and genotyping indicated that several individuals of each species were involved: in May 2013, for example, a minimum of seven pine martens and six stone martens were identified from scats found underground in the tunnels. Dietary analysis revealed that the martens were indeed preying upon the bats – mainly Daubenton's and mouse-eared – although the impact upon bat populations was not believed to be significant. Among many fascinating revelations from this study, what I find extraordinary is the confirmation that both pine and stone martens can navigate through the hazard-filled underground tunnels in total darkness to detect and predate hibernating bats successfully.

ACTIVITY PATTERNS

We have learnt that pine martens reduce their levels of activity in winter as a strategy to cope with extreme cold. Otherwise their patterns of activity are influenced by the basic needs to avoid predators and other sources of danger, to defend a territory, find a mate and rear young, and to ensure they get enough food: the last can best be achieved by timing their activity so that it coincides with when prey are most accessible and when competitors – such as the stone marten and red fox – are less active.

Although a majority of their activity occurs between dusk and dawn, pine martens are not strictly nocturnal; indeed, they are much less nocturnal than stone martens and polecats, and this may help to reduce competition for food with these other mustelids. Even in the absence of these competitors, recent camera trap evidence gathered by the VWT and others in Scotland has revealed frequent bouts of pine marten activity during daytime, including foraging bouts and other activities such as mothers moving kits between den sites.

Andrzej Zalewski's radio-tracking study in Białowieża Forest in eastern Poland revealed that over the whole year 31 per cent of pine marten activity occurred in daylight, with some marked seasonal variations: between October and March there was very little daytime activity; but over the rest of the year about half occurred in daytime, peaking in July when more than 60 per cent of activity was diurnal. Zalewski found that pine martens engaged in up to six bouts of activity in each 24-hour period, separated by short rests at night and longer rests during the day; males tended to have longer activity bouts than did females, averaging four and three hours respectively.

'GIMME SHELTER' – DENS AND RESTING SITES

Seeking elevation and insulation

Like most other carnivores, pine martens need their beauty sleep: over a whole year they typically spend an average of 60 per cent of their time resting; and in winter when the weather is poor and there are fewer jobs to do around the home range – such as mating and rearing young – this figure may exceed 80 per cent. So, access to suitable dens and resting sites is very important for pine martens, and they need to find structures that provide sufficient protection against bad weather and predators. Pine martens tend to occupy rather cold and windy parts of the northern hemisphere, so loss of body heat is a problem if they rest in exposed places. Also, their absence of a 'stink' defence makes them more vulnerable to predators than some other mustelids, so they need to rest in places where predators such as foxes cannot reach them. On top of these predation risks and thermo-energetic constraints, breeding females have to worry about finding natal den sites that provide sufficient insulation for them and their young kits when they are most vulnerable.

Thanks to their special climbing skills and preference for habitats dominated by trees, for millennia pine martens have been able to sleep and breed well out of reach of foxes in sheltered, elevated tree cavities, where the insulative properties of wood have kept generations of marten kits cosy. That was before we humans started clearing the wildwood to make space for agriculture and developed the habit of harvesting the surviving woodlands for timber at intervals. Consequently, things are very different now and, across the pine marten's Eurasian range, suitable tree cavities are much scarcer as I shall explain below, and this is especially true of Britain and Ireland. The one glowing exception is Białowieża Forest, the closest surviving approximation to the unmanaged 'wildwood' on the border between Poland and Belarus, where average tree age is 300 years.

My friend Andrzej Zalewski radio-tracked pine martens in the oldest core of Białowieża Forest and found that more than 90 per cent of their resting sites were high up in the trees. This is because tree cavities are unusually abundant due to the more natural age profile of its trees. Tree cavities are not exclusive to pine martens of course, and studies in Białowieża Forest by the Polish Academy of Sciences indicate that they are also used as breeding sites by 32 bird species, probably 11 species of bat, as well as the forest dormouse, edible dormouse, yellow-necked mouse, European red squirrel and a variety of invertebrates such as bees, wasps and beetles.

Missing cavities

The abundance of tree cavities is mainly determined by the amount of 'standing deadwood' (meaning bits of the tree that have died and started to decay) within a tree, and the older the tree the greater the volume of 'deadwood'. As a general, rule cavities in the trunk or limbs suitable for pine martens to squeeze into are rare or absent in trees that are less than a hundred years, although the humble birch tree is one exception because it has soft wood and tends to senesce at a younger age than other species (my noble surname derives from the northern English variant of birch, and denoted someone who lived by a birch tree or in a birch wood, so perhaps my ancestors also had a thing about pine martens?).

Because of the long and continuing history of harvesting our woodlands for timber, including two World Wars during the last century, the great majority of our woodland trees are less than 70 years old – even our ancient woodlands are dominated by biologically young trees, above ground at least; in fact, our oldest trees with the greatest potential to provide marten dens are mostly found outside woodlands in deer parks and field boundaries, where timber production is a lower priority. The large conifer plantations established in Britain and Ireland during the twentieth century represent good potential habitat for pine martens because they are so extensive; but the trees are commercial crops harvested frequently, so cavities suitable for pine martens are exceptionally rare.

Another exception to the rule about cavities in young trees is where species such as woodpeckers excavate their own breeding chambers suitable for pine martens to use: in Britain and Ireland our woodpeckers are scarcely big enough to build cavities suitable for pine martens to rest in, and the nest chamber is too small to accommodate a marten litter; but in continental Europe the crow-sized black woodpecker excavates a larger nesting chamber, so potential pine marten natal dens are widely available in trees across the channel.

So, in this crucial respect, woodlands in continental Europe are different from those on our islands, with tree stands of comparable age to ours having suitable den cavities for pine martens thanks to the efforts of black woodpeckers. Ecologist Scott Brainerd acknowledges that, in modern managed forests across Europe, pine martens are more or less dependent upon black woodpecker nesting chambers for successful breeding dens; and long-term studies in the Netherlands by the Werkgroep Boommarter Nederland (WBN – the Dutch Pine Marten Working Group) tend to confirm this. However, it is not all plain sailing for the pine martens because, in order to reduce the risk of predation, black woodpeckers tend to excavate their nest chambers high up in those trees – such as the typically smooth-barked beech – that pine martens find it least easy to climb.

The challenges presented by this step in the predator-prey arms race were vividly illustrated to me one spring when members of the WBN showed me a pine marten natal den some 15 metres up in a beech tree beside a forestry road that was also a well-used cycle path – we could just see the mother marten's face as she peeped sleepily out of the entrance hole. I was so keen to see her emerge that, despite the rather damp day, three of us crept back at dusk to watch the den from a downwind spot about 40 metres away. After 20 minutes we saw the mother marten emerge into the evening drizzle and descend carefully to a side-branch about eight metres above the ground. From there, after a pause to deposit a scat in the crook of the branch, she deliberately jumped to the ground, landing on the cycle path with a thump that we heard easily from our hiding place; then she shook herself down and lolloped off into the gloom. She had clearly decided that it was safer to jump rather than risk climbing down the rest of the smooth and slippery beech trunk. If a damp beech tree is so tricky for an adult marten to climb down, what hope is there for her kits when they start to explore outside the den 15 metres above the ground?

Where do pine martens sleep and breed?

With their preferred elevated tree cavities predictably scarce in Irish and British woodlands, what do pine martens use as den sites? While working for the VWT we set out to answer this via a questionnaire of Scottish naturalists and foresters, combined with scrutiny of papers and reports describing Scottish radio-tracking studies that had recorded marten dens. We gathered information on 370 Scottish pine marten dens used between 1983 and 2004, of which 70 were natal dens (sites where mother martens gave birth to their kits). We were not surprised to find that fewer than half of all dens – and less than a quarter of natal dens – were associated with trees. What did surprise us, however, was the number of natal dens that were either in buildings (44 per cent) or in other man-made structures such as bird boxes (17 per cent). This dependence of breeding females upon buildings, many of which were occupied houses, fuels much of the conflict between pine martens and people in Scotland and Ireland (see *Roof martens*, page 164). Pine martens also occupy dens in other risky places: there are recent reports from Scotland of denning in the huge stick-pile nests of large raptors such as ospreys and eagles, where even an adult marten would make a tasty snack for the avian occupants upstairs.

Den categories used by Scottish pine martens

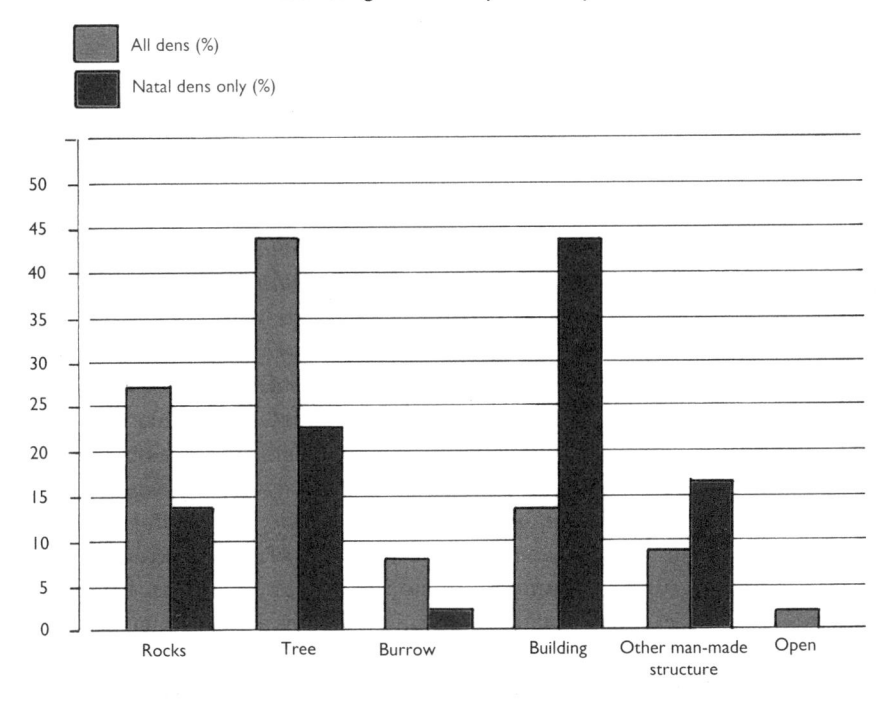

- All dens (%)
- Natal dens only (%)

Designing bedrooms and nurseries for martens

Just like the many birds and bats that use purpose-built boxes for resting and breeding – especially where we have deprived them of natural tree cavities – pine martens can be persuaded to use den boxes, but mother martens are fussy so it is critical to get the design right. My VWT colleague John Messenger designed a wooden den box that is as cunning as it is heavy (13 kilograms to be precise); it has two low-level entrances that permit some airflow through the box while minimising convection heat loss (a major problem with boxes that have their entrance holes near the top); the low level entrances are on the tree side of the box and give access to a pair of lateral internal 'chimneys' that lead up and over into a snug and well insulated central chamber that has no external joints to allow the draughts in; the size of the central chamber, in which we kindly provide wood shavings for maximum comfort, is based on the dimensions of black woodpecker nest cavities that are popular as pine marten breeding sites in continental Europe.

Pine martens simply love these wooden VWT boxes: when we checked them (under a licence from Scottish Natural Heritage) the year after we first installed ten of them in Galloway Forest, we found six had been used by pine martens and two of them contained litters of kits. Thanks to FES there are now 50 of these VWT boxes spread about Galloway Forest. They have been used for breeding in most years, and are also frequently used as over-winter den sites by resident adult martens, so I am convinced that they contribute to improved breeding success and over-winter survival of pine martens in a forest where natural tree cavities are effectively absent. Because the VWT has made details of their design and construction freely available via their website, many people have installed these boxes elsewhere in Ireland, Scotland and now Wales.

The one hefty (literally!) flaw with the VWT box is its large size and weight, meaning that it needs to be installed on a large tree – the sort of tree that is typically due for felling in connection with timber production in modern forests. Consequently, in order to ensure that the VWT boxes can enjoy a good few undisturbed years, the places where they can be installed in a commercial forest are rather few and far between, and these usually involve stands of large trees set aside from harvesting for some reason and designated for 'long-term retention'. To free us from this constraint we needed a smaller, lighter box – equally attractive to pine martens – that could be installed on younger trees almost anywhere in a commercial forest. My friend John Martin sourced new materials and produced his Galloway Lite den box, which elegantly combines a robust plastic exterior with a modular plywood interior, and a very sheltered entrance hole facing the tree trunk; and its weight and cost is a quarter of that of the VWT box. While struggling to come to terms with a name that evokes a Scottish beer, cigarette or contraceptive more than a bedroom for pine martens, we installed 50 Galloway Lites at even spacing across one part of Galloway Forest in 2014. The pine martens loved these ones too, and almost half showed signs of occupancy in the year following their installation; and by the third year over three-quarters had been used.

Pine martens commonly express their gratitude by using the den box lids as toilets, enabling us to detect a well-used box from some distance away by spotting the scats on top through binoculars. When a breeding female occupies a box for several weeks, huge piles of scats may accumulate on the lid; but occasionally a mother leaves no visible scats either on the box lid or on the ground beneath (nor inside the box), reminding us that there are individual differences in behaviour within a marten population.

Installation of a Galloway Lite pine marten den box (normally these are deployed on trees with abundant side branches beneath the box to assist climbing by young martens).

FIELD SIGNS

Where a pine marten population is well established, the most abundant and detectable field signs are the droppings – called scats – that the animals deposit in many prominent places around their home ranges for the purpose of scent-based communication; these are described at (hideous) length in *The Joy of Scats* below.

After scats, footprints are the next-best field sign to look for. Where snow covers the ground pine martens cannot avoid leaving footprints; but in snow-free places and seasons prints are surprisingly difficult to find because of the martens' cat-like fastidious avoidance of mud. Also cat-like is the common absence – except in deep mud or snow – of claw marks in marten prints because of their habit of holding their claws raised slightly above the substrate they walk on; marten prints may also look cat-like because they commonly show only four of the five toes; but marten prints tend to be larger than domestic cat prints, with more space between the toe pads and the arc-like, four-lobed palm pads behind (in cats the palm pad is a solid, near-triangular block compared with the marten's delicately lobed arc).

Underside of pine marten feet in winter pelage, drawn from photographs taken in the west of Scotland by John Martin: right hind foot (on left) showing thick fur partly obscuring small toe pads; right fore foot (on right) showing longer claws and pads less obscured by fur.

PINE MARTENS | FIELD SIGNS

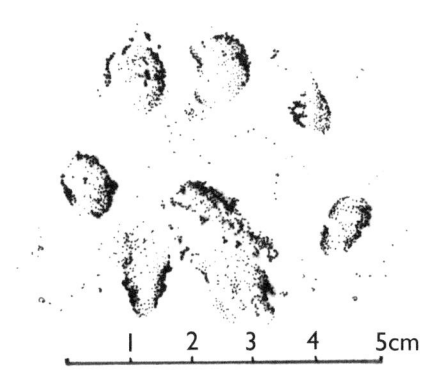

Pine marten footprint (probably right fore foot without heel pad showing) in shallow mud, showing palm pad and all five toe pads but no claw marks.

The size of marten footprints varies greatly in relation to the softness of the substrate and the age, gender and speed of movement of the animal leaving them. There are differences in the size and shape of the forefeet and hind feet that are reflected in the prints: the presence of a small proximal heel pad at the rear of each forefoot means that forefoot prints tend to be more elongated than the hind foot prints, which are about as long as they are wide; another difference is the greater furriness of the hind feet in winter pelage, which results in hind foot prints being more fuzzy and indistinct than their forefoot counterparts in winter. The best guide to the size of marten prints is from measurements taken by Rob Strachan and shown in the table below.

Age and gender	Forefoot print	Hind foot print
Adult female	40 mm wide x 45 mm long	42 mm wide x 42 mm long
Adult male	55 mm wide x 65 mm long	55 mm wide x 55 mm long

Measurements of pine marten footprints in firm mud made in Scotland by the late Rob Strachan; note that the forefoot print lengths include the small heel pad (if this pad does not show, the prints are shorter in length); and the measurements given are for prints in which all five toes are visible (where only four toes show, which is not unusual, the prints are less wide).

Faster-moving pine martens typically move with a lollopy, bounding gait that tends to leave the footprints in clumps of four. The stride length varies with the nature of the substrate, the terrain and speed of the animal: so, on firm, flat ground the footprint clumps may be 75 to 90 centimetres apart, while in deep loose snow the gap may be only 55 to 70 centimetres.

Field signs can be found at well-used pine marten dens, such as claw-marks on tree trunks and branches, dislodged or worn bark and moss, accumulations of scats and prey remains, and hairs trapped in rough wood around den entrances. Dutch ecologists used to search for the widely spaced marten claw-marks on trees (usually only four of the five claws left a mark), but the marks left by stone and pine martens could not be distinguished, so instead they searched for woodpecker holes with marten scats on the ground beneath. Bear in mind that occupied den sites are protected from disturbance by law, so it is best not to approach such sites closely unless you have the relevant licence.

One final field sign to be aware of is the inter-canine distance (ICD) that may be reflected in the tooth-marks found on some prey killed or certain foods eaten by a pine marten. Most of the mustelids of Britain and Ireland have a different-sized gap between their canine teeth (although mink and polecats are very similar in this respect) and this can be used to guess which species was involved: for example, pine martens use the characteristic mustelid 'killer bite' around the head or neck area of larger prey such as rabbits and large birds; by skinning the carcass and examining the skin side without fur or feathers one can sometimes measure the distance between the paired puncture marks left by the canine teeth; and predated large birds' eggs may carry similar evidence. Note that the upper canines tend to have a greater distance between their tips than the lower ones; and because of sexual dimorphism the females of each mustelid have slightly smaller ICDs. The table below shows typical male pine marten ICDs (measured from tooth tip to tip) with those of a polecat for comparison.

	Upper inter-canine distance	Lower inter-canine distance
Adult male pine marten	16 mm	13 mm
Adult male polecat	11 mm	9.5 mm

THE JOY OF SCATS

Heaven-scent!
We mammal-workers are renowned for our obsession with dung; this is mainly because we glean so much information from the pungently precious parcels left behind by our typically elusive study animals. In this respect, carnivore biologists are top of the tree because finding a scat (as carnivore poo is called) is usually the closest we get to our quarry, and marten-workers take this faecal frenzy to new heights: whenever two or more are gathered together their reverential discussions of scat morphology and scent can fill a room for hours, with an unsettling resemblance to a wine-tasting session (although there is usually less tasting and spitting); and out in the field they spend a lot of time kneeling nose to ground over fresh scats, or passing scat-plastered sticks from nose to nose in search of agreement on whose bottom the poo came from and when. Of course, scats are important to the pine martens too, for they are the scented social media facilitating chemical communication between individuals.

Although I accept that the description of scent is a subjective matter – so not everyone will agree with me – the delicate, musky-sweet scent of a fresh pine marten scat merely adds to the appeal of this charming mammal and sets it apart from those mustelid relatives that have based their reputations on the production of more pungent poo. However, among my many scat-sniffing friends it has proved surprisingly difficult to agree upon a single definition of the scent: the late, great Rob Strachan likened it to the smell of Parma Violets (violet-tasting purple sweets made in Derbyshire by Swizzels Matlow) with a hint of musk; some list cranberry sauce and fresh-mown hay as dominant components; Laura Kubasiewicz leans towards a combination of marmite and green tea; others detect an aromatic quality, or a fishy-ness, and even a chemical tang suggestive of dishwasher tablets; and most eloquent of all is Huw Denman's 'Lapsang Souchong tea with a hint of rotting seaweed, more sweet than smoky'. All agree that the scent of fresh marten scats is not unpleasant and never makes you gag, and for that we can be truly thankful. Also, marten scats don't always smell the same and this variability – not necessarily determined by their diverse contents – goes some way to explain the lack of agreement on a single description of the scent.

Variations in form, texture and colour

As we should expect from an omnivore with a very broad diet and a tendency to gyrate its bottom while defaecating (see section on the hip-wiggle, page 86), the pine marten produces scats that vary considerably in size, shape, texture and colour. In the face of such scientifically inconvenient diversity one or two brave souls have tried to produce a classification system, and even to define a 'typical' marten scat, if such a thing exists. Although such efforts to impose order are doomed in my view, nevertheless I celebrate the sensual-sounding 'Moist Classic' coined by Laura Kubasiewicz: this is a long, slim, near-black, sticky and shiny creation strangely reminiscent of the big black slugs that ravage our garden plants (though slightly less mobile and without the eyes on stalks); in fact slugs frequently consume pine marten scats as a welcome change from dog poo, so perhaps we should not be too surprised if some of them end up looking like them!

Of course, most marten scats don't look like the 'sluggy' Moist Classic:

some land as piles of fragmented sections, runny splodges or coiled 'walnut whips', and some depart wildly from the simple grey-black-brown colour chart; but the variations in colour and texture are far from random – they are directly linked to the geographical and seasonal changes in the nature of marten food consumed (we shall explore these dietary details elsewhere). One of the delights of studying pine martens lies in the opportunities to witness the ever-changing kaleidoscope of scats through the year. Whilst you cannot quite set your clock by them, I can at least guess which month I am in by the colour and texture of the marten scats I find – a useful skill if one is stranded in a forest without a calendar!

Typically we start the year with matt grey-black scats full of late-winter voles, with their convoluted twistings of fur, delicate bone fragments and the occasional zig-zag molar tooth; then on to the greyish-green scats of spring, either sticky with amphibian remains such as the 'double-barrelled' limb bones of frogs, or spiky with the white-tipped quills of fledgling birds; early summer brings the first injection of true colour in the form of scats jewel-encrusted with the iridescent blue-black wing cases of woodland beetles; late summer and autumn produces an explosion of colours as martens feast on fruit and their scats sometimes become predictably sloppy and dotted with pips and stones, with the reds, blues, ferrous browns, mauves and purples of bilberries, raspberries, blackberries and wild cherries, and the bright orange of rowan berries (curiously rowan berries in marten scats appear much as they do on the trees that produce them, but presumably some nutritional benefit is derived as they pass through the gut apparently unchanged); autumn is also when martens raid the nests of wild bumble bees, producing bizarre beige-yellow scats with the smooth texture of putty (reminding me of some primitive marine Annelid worm) – comprising the remains of bee larvae and fragments of honeycomb – and dotted with occasional darker bits of adult bee; winter sees the return of monochrome scats filled with rodent fur and, depending upon where the nearest bird-feeding station is, chunky brown and cream scats full of well-chewed peanuts; and martens scavenge human left-overs too – one Scottish scat was full of chewing gum!

I have tried to reflect some of this diversity in the scat-photo-montage opposite page 67. Having accepted that there is no such thing as a typical marten scat it seems foolish to offer any information on scat dimensions.

However, if you are one of those for whom size really does matter, most elongate pine marten scats are 10–13 millimetres wide and 80–120 millimetres long (following all the curves and twists). Of course, this excludes those scats at the extremes of the size range, like the squitty ones as little as 7 x 70 millimetres; and the occasional eye-watering Bratwurst at 14 x 150 millimetres (my personal length record for a marten scat is 190 millimetres, though I don't like to boast about it).

If you want to get your eye in – and your nose, of course, for a good sniff is compulsory – there are many places in Scotland and Ireland where you are guaranteed to find thrilling numbers of pine marten scats: one of my favourite spots is the fabulous Atlantic oak woodland at Ariundle National Nature Reserve near Strontian in Argyll, Scotland, where a gentle stroll around the nature trail will be punctuated by 15–20 encounters with a fresh marten scat deposited on the trail itself; and in Ireland there are similar dead-cert scat detection opportunities at Dromore Wood near Ennis in County Clare, and at the National Trust's Crom Estate on the shores of Upper Lough Erne in County Fermanagh.

The hip-wiggle (please don't try this at home!)

One of the benefits of the wide scale use of camera traps to record video footage of wildlife is the insights they offer into aspects of mammal behaviour that are otherwise very difficult to observe. The VWT's use of camera traps to record pine marten behaviour in Scottish forests has recorded abundant footage that explains why most marten scats are deposited in interesting curvy shapes. For the footage shows that most pine martens do not keep their bottoms still as they defaecate; instead they perform a delicate 'hip-wiggle' that involves a marten standing still with its hind legs well separated and the tail slightly raised, while it moves its hips from side to side, or gyrating in a circle, as a scat is produced; and we see the same movement during urination. Depending upon the complexity and duration of the wiggle, and upon the length, consistency and fragility of the faecal material, each scat lands in a variety of wavy, coiled, curved, looped and/or fragmented shapes.

There is an artistic consequence of the hip wiggle that makes me smile and adds yet more to the pine marten's appeal: while undertaking scat surveys I have found many faecal specimens in the shape of startlingly perfect letters and numbers including 'u', 'o', 'v', 'c', 'e', 's', '8', '6', '9' and '2' (yes I do have quite a large collection) as well as symbols like question marks, ampersands and less recognisable hieroglyphics. In fact, at the end of a hard day's surveying it sometimes felt as if some creative force was guiding the martens' bottoms, and even that the martens were using their 'faecal art' to send me some kind of written message (yes, I need to stay in more!). Whatever, for me the hip-wiggle is part of the pine marten's signature, both literally and figuratively, which helps me to separate its scats from those of less anally creative carnivores. For example, foxes keep their bums relatively still as they poo, so their simple scats lack the delicately curvy shapes produced by the martens.

Of course, we have to ask why pine martens do the hip-wiggle? Normally there is some adaptive value (meaning that it contributes to survival and/or breeding success in some way) to such patterns of behaviour. Does the wiggle help to squeeze something extra out of the anal scent glands? Do interesting 'curvy' scats and 'wiggly' wee distribute scent more effectively than boring straight ones? Perhaps the wiggle helps to keep the martens' precious fur clean as a scat comes out? Or does it simply feel good to wiggle as you poo? It is urgent that we find answers to these crucial questions through diligent research, and I look forward to reading a delicately titled paper that lays the (faecal) matter to rest in the near future.

Scats for surveys

Although martens leave many of their scats at their dens, resting sites and in other secretive places, a proportion of them are deposited deliberately and strategically for other martens to find as a part of their scent-based communication system (see *Marten communications*, page 116). In common with some other carnivores, pine martens use woodland tracks, rides, paths and roads for this 'social' scatting. Consequently, finding and counting scats along woodland tracks has been the basis for pine marten surveys, especially in Britain and Ireland, ever since Jim Lockie suggested in the 1960s that there could be a link between the numbers of scats he found on his walks around Beinn Eighe National Nature Reserve and the number of pine martens that produced them. This helpful toilet behaviour is just one of many reasons why marten scats are so useful to surveyors, because it means that any system of tracks and paths through suitable habitat will likely reveal the presence of martens, provided that the population is sufficiently well-established for its members to need to communicate with each other and defend their territories. However, where martens are present but the population is not well established one may find no scats at all; so, to coin the astronomers' phrase 'an absence of evidence is not evidence of absence'.

Pine marten scat surveys involve searching a series of standard transects of a kilometre or more in length – 1.5 kilometres is currently the favoured transect length for surveys in Britain and Ireland – along tracks through suitable habitat (usually woodland or forestry plantation), with a count being kept of the number of marten scats found. One or two surveyors walk slowly – 4 kilometres per hour works well for me (colleagues describe my progress as a 'focused bimble') – along the transect scanning the ground ahead for anything that looks like a marten scat. This approach works well so long as we are confident that scats are correctly identified (this is where the Gene-genies come in, as we shall see below) and that we don't try to make unsafe assumptions about the patterns of scat abundance that we record.

We should not ignore the unsung contribution of forestry engineers to the successful operation of pine marten scat surveys. I frequently say a grateful 'hurrah' to them for building and maintaining a magnificent network of linear pine marten toilets throughout their publically accessible forests that, fortuitously, also allow safe access for we marten surveyors and the occasional timber lorry. And it begs the interesting question as to where pine martens would deposit their 'social' scats in the absence of forest tracks: presumably along deer paths and other animal trails?

As well as reflecting marten activity to some degree, the number of marten scats detected on transects is influenced by several non-marten factors. For example, the nature of the track surface – rough, dark and stony or smooth, pale and sandy – may affect the visibility of scats, as does the nature and extent of vegetation on the track; high levels of vehicle use may destroy scats soon after they are deposited, and so too may heavy rain and slug or beetle activity (some invertebrates adore the taste of fresh marten scats); and some surveyors are simply better at spotting scats than others. Finally, where scenting conditions are suitable, a scat detection dog may find scats that we humans miss.

It is tempting to assume that the number of marten scats we find is related in some way to the number of pine martens present in a forest. Actually, no clear relationship exists because the numbers of detectable scats on woodland tracks reflect patterns of social activity and communication among martens rather than their abundance. We know this because local scat abundance varies markedly in both space and time within the same block of forest: Peter Turner found that certain tracks through Portlaw Woods in Waterford tended to have high scat densities because they coincided with the boundaries between marten territories where neighbours placed many scats in connection with territorial defence, while similar tracks nearby had very few or no scats because they lay well within an occupied territory where territorial marking was pretty pointless. As an example of seasonal variation, Kathy Velander's scat surveys in the Scottish Highlands for Britain's first systematic study of pine marten distribution revealed that scat abundance may vary as much as 100-fold in the same forest between July (12 scats per kilometre) and January (0.1 scats per kilometre) because of variations in marten activity (July is in the mating season).

Study area	Season	Mean number of scats per 1-km transect
Scottish Lowlands		
Galloway Forest	Spring	1.9
Galloway Forest	Autumn	3.5
Scottish Highlands		
Strathglass	Spring	5.4
Urquhart	Spring	9
Boblainy	Spring	2
Black Isle	Spring	14.1
Contin	Spring	6.2
Morangie	Spring	9.7

Typical densities of pine marten scats recorded along tracks in Scottish forests during the period 2010 to 2015. (Data supplied by the VWT, Myotismart and Swift Ecology)

The best evidence against any link between scat abundance and the number of martens comes from the VWT's work in the Scottish Highlands in 2015 and 2016, where systematic scat surveys were followed by live-trapping martens in the same year at the same sites using a constant-effort approach: there was no relationship between the number of pine martens trapped and the number of scats found at the same site.

Scat detection dogs

Dogs have a sense of smell that is vastly more acute than our own, and this special power has been harnessed by some biologists to turn dogs into scat detection assistants during surveys for elusive carnivores such as pine martens. Crucial to achieving this canine aid is to train a dog to associate a particular scent with enthusiastic praise and a swift reward in the form of a game with a favourite toy (food treats don't make good rewards because greedy dogs tell lies!). Many things can go wrong during the training process, of course, and much depends on the dog's personality and how keenly it is motivated to search when directed, to please its owner and to soak up his or her praise and the rewards offered. Nevertheless, most dogs, if trained thoughtfully with an emphasis on encouragement and fun, can become scat detectors.

Guided by my supremely patient friend John Martin – who knows more about training witless dog-owners than anyone I have ever met (for it is the owners that really need the training, not the dogs) – I have enjoyed teaching two of our pet dogs to become nearly as excited as I am by the scent of pine martens and their excretions. The most recent is Dooley, a Labrador-lurcher cross, who quickly realised that by finding a pine marten scat and smiling a bit he could make me whoop with joy and throw his favourite tennis ball an extraordinarily long way for him to chase. Here is not the place to describe the training process in detail, but I am keen to share some of the benefits of involving a dog in surveys to confirm the presence of pine martens.

As explained above, in Britain and Ireland the low-cost approach to detecting pine martens in a forest involves searching lengths of forest track for scats. We human surveyors have only our eyesight to rely upon, and sometimes the weather or track conditions are such that only a low proportion of scats is clearly visible to us. Where scats are scarce, this carries the risk of false negatives – meaning that marten scats are present in low numbers on a transect but we fail to spot any of them. Therefore, if we can involve a trained dog to combine its sense of smell with our eyesight we can reduce the risk of false negatives. Of course, there are situations where a dog's sense of smell cannot help us, such as when scats are so old or rain-washed that there is no detectable scent left, or when the weather is too cold, dry or windy for any scent to be detectable. But where fresh scats are present and the weather is right (warm, damp and wind-free is best, and early in the day because scent deteriorates over time) a dog can be a superb addition to a scat survey team.

I remember one drizzly transect in Galloway Forest – where it does rain a bit – on a rough, dark, stony track (perfect camouflage for scats) in still, warm, humid conditions (perfect for detecting scent) when Dooley outscored me by four to one because he could smell the fresh scats that my eyes could not pick out among the similar-coloured stones. Dooley does not provide a very clear indication when he has found a marten scat (that is due to my incompetence as a trainer rather than any failure on his part), but he does give a long and concentrated sniff followed by a particular look in my direction that, although quite subtle, I have learnt to recognise over the years I have been assisting him with pine marten surveys (and after his crushing victory on the Galloway transect I swear he walked with an extra swagger for the rest of the day).

Another situation in which a detection dog can help is where fresh scats have been crushed by vehicle wheels passing along a transect so that they are no longer visible or recognisable to a human surveyor. On a transect in Whitelee Forest in East Renfrewshire in 2013, as part of a pine marten distribution survey of southern Scotland, Dooley gave me 'the look' at two smears of browny-grey gunk about a metre apart on gritty mud of the same colour in a fresh tyre track; he also dipped his shoulder as if to roll on them, which is one of his more demonstrative indications that he has found marten scent. Normally I would never have collected such unlikely looking material even if I had spotted it, but because of Dooley's confident reaction, and because I had found little else resembling marten scats on that transect or anywhere else that day, I scooped each smear into a separate bag and they were sent off to the Gene-genies in Waterford for DNA testing.

When I later met Catherine O'Reilly (chief Gene-genie) she was full of praise for the canine member of our team: both the scats were so fresh – with the DNA abundant and in good condition – that she had easily confirmed them as being from a pine marten; furthermore, the DNA revealed that two individuals were involved because one scat was from a female and the other from a male, so probably an example of counter-marking where each left a scented faecal message for the other. On analysing the survey results it emerged that the Whitelee Forest transect was the only DNA-positive one in the entire hectad (a 10 km by 10 km square), and that in turn was the only DNA-positive hectad in that part of Scotland. So, thanks to Dooley's nose, the survey had confirmed the presence of two pine martens in an area where the species had not been recorded in recent times.

When working on pine marten surveys with a scat detection dog, a problem arises from the martens' habit of leaving some of their scent by rubbing their glands or dribbling urine on the ground or objects such as stones and logs, or in places where another marten has left scent. We know from camera trap video footage how often martens mark their surroundings in this way, so we should expect that a trained dog will frequently detect scent that is not associated with a scat. Many times during surveys, I have noticed Dooley giving me 'the look' in the absence of any visible sign to encourage me to offer praise and reward. In such cases I can only imagine his frustration as he tries to convey the message 'it's marten scent you blithering idiot – can't you smell it? Plonker!' I feel bad that such detections have to go unrewarded.

The work of the Gene-genies
It will already be obvious that geneticists have made huge contributions to our understanding of the pine marten's origins and evolution, its phylogeography and taxonomic relationships. By enabling us to identify individuals via their unique genotypes, they have given us new insights into who lives where and how populations tick over; and by extracting DNA from all sorts of gunk they have improved the rigour of our surveys, especially those based on non-invasive methods such as hair sampling and scat detection.

My first insight into the thrilling underworld of pine marten genetics came when the VWT engaged Angus Davison of Nottingham University to advance our limited knowledge of pine marten phylogeography. He also helped us in 1999 with a blind trial of experienced marten scat surveyors to see how accurate their field identification of scats really was. Three brave souls collected marten scats from Galloway Forest and submitted them to Angus for DNA analysis to determine which mammal had actually produced them: surprisingly, 18 per cent of scats identified as 'marten' were actually from foxes, with individual surveyor error rates ranging from 9 to 29 per cent.

This was a worrying discovery, especially given the faith invested since 1980 in surveyors' ability to identify scats correctly during pine marten surveys (upon which national population assessments were based). We published our findings in the *Journal of Zoology* in a paper entitled 'On the origin of faeces: morphological versus molecular methods for surveying rare carnivores from their scats' (the journal initially rejected our suggested title on the grounds that it might be seen as flippant treatment of Darwin's legacy, but we stood firm). Ever since, genetic verification of scats has become a standard part of pine marten surveys in Britain and Ireland.

THE PINE MARTEN'S YEAR

Like all wild mammals, the pine marten's social life, patterns of behaviour and levels of activity are heavily influenced by changing hormone levels, prey availability, climatic extremes, mating activity, and the demands of rearing young and establishing and then defending a territory. The table below is a simple summary of what is happening (or not happening!) marten-wise in each month of the year.

Jan	Activity levels are low and martens spend a lot of time resting in dens.
Feb	Pregnancy starts with implantation of blastocysts; pregnant females select natal dens that offer good shelter, insulation and protection from predators; young born the previous year disperse.
Mar	More sub-adult dispersal; many litters born in mid- to late March.
Apr	More litters born; moult starts in adults around the muzzle, with pale fluffy winter coat replaced by short, dark summer coat; adult activity increases.
May	Marten kits' eyes open and weaning starts, so mothers bring fresh prey to natal dens; kits first appear at den entrances in late May (and sometimes fall out!), so mother martens may move their kits to new den sites where they can learn to climb safely.
Jun	Marten kits grow in confidence, become more boisterous in their play and follow their mothers on hunting trips away from the natal den; mating activity starts, with adult males visiting mothers at their den sites.
Jul	By mid-July the kits appear as big as their mothers and begin to move around her home range independently; the mating season continues, with adult males travelling widely in search of oestrus females.

Aug	Mating season comes to an end; kits become independent but still tolerated within mother's home range; martens eat a lot of fruit and insects.
Sep	Juveniles reach adult size but still stick together within mum's home range.
Oct	Moult starts, with long, fluffy winter pelage replacing summer coat; activity levels start to reduce.
Nov	Martens spend less time out foraging and more time in dens resting.
Dec	As above.

SOCIAL LIFE AND HOME RANGE BEHAVIOUR

Territoriality
Pine martens exhibit what is called 'intrasexual territoriality', which means that each adult tries to occupy a separate area – called a home range or territory – in which overlap with members of the same sex is not tolerated. So, while there is usually extensive range overlap between males and females, there is rarely any overlap between adults of the same gender. This all sounds very simple, well organised and, perhaps, just a tiny bit boring. However, in the years since David Balharry's ground-breaking radio-tracking study in the rugged north-west Highlands of Scotland in the late 1980s, which led him to conclude that the species was hamstrung by an inflexible social organisation, we have been learning that the pine martens' social lives are a bit more interesting than we once thought.

Home range sizes
We now know that there are huge variations – at least ten-fold – in the average size of home ranges occupied by pine martens within Britain and Ireland, and these differences are related closely to habitat quality and, especially, food availability: the best quality habitats provide a great diversity and biomass of food, so home ranges don't need to be so large. For example, the table below shows that, within Scotland, average home ranges sizes vary between 33 square kilometres for males and 11 square kilometres for females in the poorest habitat in upland monoculture conifer plantations, down to as little as three square kilometres for males and less than one square kilometre for females in lowland mixed conifer plantations. In most studies males occupied home ranges that were, on average, 1.5 to 3 times larger than those of the females. This is partly because male martens are larger than females and so have greater energy needs; it is also because a larger home range enables each male to maintain contact with more females, so males choose to occupy larger ranges because of their associated reproductive benefits.

Study area	Habitat	Mean male home range size (square kilometres)	Mean female home range size (square kilometres)	Lead researcher and main decade of study
Kinlochewe, north-west Scotland	Open mountain with small woodlands	23.63	8.83	D. Balharry 1980s
Strathglass, north-west Scotland	Mixed valley-side woodland	6.28	3.57	D. Balharry 1990s
Novar Forest, northern Scotland	Lowland mixed conifer plantation	3.04	2.03	E. Halliwell 1990s
Morangie Forest, northern Scotland	Lowland mixed conifer plantation	5.63	0.70	F. Caryl 2000s
Glen Trool, south-west Scotland	Lowland mixed conifer plantation	8.36	4.52	P. Bright 1990s
Minnoch, south-west Scotland	Upland spruce plantation	32.86	10.61	P. Bright 1990s
Killavoggy, County Leitrim, Republic of Ireland	Upland conifer plantations	1.71	0.99	D. O'Mahony 2000s

Home range sizes of pine martens derived from radio-tracking studies in Scotland and Ireland.

Pine marten home ranges in Ireland are typically much smaller than those recorded in Scotland and in many other parts of Europe. For example, Declan O'Mahony's study in County Leitrim revealed average home ranges of less than two square kilometres in upland conifer plantations – so rather poor habitat – when compared with the monstrous ranges in similar habitat in Scotland. A 1970s live-trapping study by Paddy O'Sullivan in lowland broad-leaved woodland – high quality habitat – at Dromore in County Clare predictably revealed even smaller home ranges: O'Sullivan found that the 1.4 square kilometre Dromore Wood supported 10– 12 adult pine martens, with the largest male home range only 0.44 square kilometres. Thanks to my persuasive VWT colleague Kate McAney, I was able to join Paddy O'Sullivan on a live-trapping session there one May in the mid-1990s: I was truly amazed when, using 20 traps in just one small part of the wood, he caught five adult pine martens on the first night.

The reasons why Irish pine martens are content to occupy such small home ranges relative to those in the rest of Europe must be partly due to the mild and humid conditions at the western fringe of their global distribution, where 'life is easy' in the absence of climatic extremes, and abundant and easily gathered fruit and insects dominate the martens' diets. Another possible influence on pine marten home range size is the sparse nature of the carnivore community in Ireland, where potential competitors like the weasel, wildcat, polecat and stone marten are all absent; this suggests that pine martens in Ireland have access to a greater share of the food available than they do in the rest of Europe, so can make do with smaller home ranges.

Pine martens don't make equal use of all parts of their home ranges; rather, they tend to concentrate their time in the best foraging habitat (already examined in the section above on *Woodland specialist or habitat generalist?*, page 67). Pine martens usually have one or two favourite patches known as 'core areas', and the locations and sizes of these vary seasonally in response to changing food availability. O'Mahony found that these core areas – defined by concentrations of 50 per cent of radio-locations (so where a marten spends about half of its time) – typically represent 23 per cent of male and 45 per cent of female home ranges; they may be as small as 10 hectares (although on average they were about

38 hectares for both genders in Ireland); and they tend to be larger in spring/summer than in autumn/winter.

Social martens
Beyond the flexibility in size and usage patterns of home ranges revealed by radio-tracking, there is recent evidence of a richer social life than we would normally associate with a supposedly solitary mustelid like the pine marten. There is a neighbourly tolerance between adults whose home ranges overlap, and recent studies suggest that tolerance doesn't occur only between martens of different genders as previously believed: O'Mahony found four cases of home range overlap between radio-collared adult male pine martens in his County Leitrim study, with an average of 12 per cent and a maximum of 25 per cent range overlap between individuals.

Video recordings from inside a Scottish den box – revealed via the Pine Marten Diaries on Facebook – have shown us that wild adult pine martens may sometimes share resting sites outside the mating season. Similarly, a radio-tracking study in the west of Scotland by Rob Coope recorded an adult male and female marten bunking up together in a den site in late winter; Coope also found that, when he recaptured his animals, on some of them the radio collars had been gently chewed by other martens, suggesting that there had been mutual grooming (rather than fighting) between some of the animals in his study area.

Some of this sociability among pine martens may arise because of the delayed dispersal of juveniles and the extended sub-adult phase reported in some studies of this relatively long-lived mustelid (see *The male 'teenage' phase*, page 130). This means that over the winter period fully adult pine martens may tolerate the presence of adult-sized but subdominant youngsters before they disperse in early spring to find territories of their own; and sub-adult siblings may hang out together and share resting sites as they did when they were much younger.

Martelism
Another example of pine martens apparently softening their innate territoriality occurs when they are faced with an abundant food resource that is effectively undefendable. This brand of sensible social flexibility has been dubbed 'martelism' by Erkki Pullianen, who reported it from

Finland, on the northern fringes of the pine marten's global range, where several individuals were observed to share ungulate carcasses without aggression. The same type of tolerant food-sharing is probably involved where several different pine martens visit a well-established feeding station supplied by we humans, although we know that these are not entirely aggression-free zones.

FORAGING AND FOOD

A multi-skilled omnivore
The pine marten's acute senses, climbing skills, long, slim shape and its preference for diverse wooded habitats means that it can gain access to a very wide range of food. Powerful senses of hearing and smell help a pine marten to detect small rodents and amphibians moving beneath the leaf litter on the woodland floor; climbing trees and squeezing into tree holes enables it to reach the places used for resting, roosting, nesting and breeding by a variety of birds, arboreal mammals and invertebrates; and climbing trees and shrubs also ensures that, in the right season, honey, fruit and nuts can follow a protein-rich first course. And in those countries, such as Britain and Ireland, where the stone marten is absent as a competitor, pine martens are free to forage in more open habitats and close to human habitations that would otherwise be off limits. In Ireland's County Wexford Dominic Berridge was fortunate to witness a pine marten displaying its extraordinary climbing skills in his open-fronted garage one summer: the animal climbed upside down, up and along the underside of one of the sloping rafters supporting the garage roof, in order to reach a swallow's nest at the apex, where it reached over its shoulder to grab a mouthful of nestlings before descending down the rafter to eat them in the relative comfort of Dominic's log pile.

As well as being acrobatic, pine martens can be tough in pursuit of food: in late summer they frequently raid the nests of bees and wasps, presumably enduring stings in order to get at the honey and grubs; and I have seen amazing camera trap footage of a Belgian pine marten raiding the nest of a black stork high up a tree: one of the adult storks repeatedly stabs the marten with its beak as it attempts to steal the eggs; at one point the marten falls more than 20 metres to the ground, only to climb all the way back up to continue its eggy raid. Pine martens are even not averse to swimming in search of a good meal, as observed by David Bavin in the Flow Country of northern Scotland where one marten swam 30 metres to an island to predate the nest of a black-throated diver.

There is even evidence of pine martens catching fish in small pools in upland streams: a dietary study of pine martens and American mink by N. V. Kiselva in the montane forests of the Southern Urals found that fish made up 5.4 per cent of the former's diet compared with 12.7 per cent of the latter's. The diets of the two mustelids overlapped substantially, especially in respect of the consumption of small rodents and insects; the main difference – which helped them to avoid serious competition – was that fruit made up some 30 per cent of the pine marten's diet yet did not feature in the mink's diet.

So, rather like the red fox, pine martens are highly omnivorous and consume an ever-changing diet as food availability shifts through the seasons and from place to place. In fact, the diets of foxes and martens overlap so much that they frequently compete for the same resources, and this may explain why foxes show aggression towards martens and may even kill them as infuriating competitors.

The pine martens of Białowieża Forest

Before we examine the feeding ecology of pine martens in Britain and Ireland, it is useful to consider how they would have behaved before our ancestors felled the vast European wildwood. They converted most of it to open farmland and regularly harvested the remaining fragments for timber and firewood. Fortunately, an area of woodland that retains many of the characteristics of the ancient wildwood has survived in the primeval core of Białowieża Forest – now a National Park and UNESCO World Heritage Site – on the border between Belarus and Poland. My friend Andrzej Zalewski studied pine martens in the Polish part of the forest in the 1990s. His observations give us the best modern indication as to how pine martens probably behaved before we humans began to interfere with their environment and influence their ecology.

Zalewski tracked the Białowieża pine martens' changing diet through the seasons and found that, although woodland rodents like the bank vole and yellow-necked mouse were the dominant component and constantly present at 40–90 per cent (with an annual average of 60 per cent of biomass consumed), their contribution varied both seasonally and annually in response to cycles in rodent abundance and snow cover (see below). Because of their generalist foraging – enabling them to switch to other foods as a buffer when woodland rodents were scarce or inaccessible – the Białowieża pine martens avoided the population booms and crashes shown by some predators with greater dependence upon fluctuating prey (the lynx and snowshoe hare cycle in Canada being the textbook example).

Nevertheless, Zalewski did find some evidence of a numerical response to fluctuating rodent numbers in the Białowieża pine martens: the woodland rodents reached peak populations every six to nine years following an especially heavy year of tree seed production (meaning extra rodent food so lots of rodent breeding) by the oaks, hornbeams and maples that dominated the forest; in turn, pine marten numbers increased in the year following a rodent peak, with the time lag caused by the marten's delayed implantation. So, thanks to tree seed production driving changes in woodland rodent abundance, pine marten population density fluctuated, albeit with a time lag, between four and eight animals per 10 square kilometres in Białowieża Forest. (Further north in Fennoscandia, Jan Olof Helldin and Erik Lindström found that pine martens showed a weaker numerical response to vole cycles than did predators such as foxes, stoats and weasels. They explained this in terms of the pine marten's broader diet that reduced its vole-dependency compared with the other predators; and also, the pine marten's low reproductive rate made it less able to respond swiftly to the short vole cycle periodicity of 3–4 years).

While foraging on the ground for rodents (and amphibians such as frogs), which occurred mostly in spring and autumn, Zalewski's pine martens travelled on average seven kilometres per day; and they showed a preference for areas of forest with an abundance of fallen tree trunks that they used for travelling along and hunting beneath. In spring and summer the Białowieża pine martens used their climbing skills to search tree holes for birds' nests (to eat eggs and nestlings), and the nests of wild bees and wasps (for their larvae and honey). In autumn, they frequently climbed trees and bushes for rowan berries and hazelnuts, as well as feasting on fungi, bilberries and raspberries closer to the ground.

Winter in Białowieża is a tough time for pine martens, with very low air temperatures sapping their body heat, and populations of their staple rodents declining and becoming less accessible due to thick snow. In response to these wintry constraints, the martens increased their consumption of carrion by following the trails of lynx and wolves to pick at their kills of deer and wild boar. Zalewski also found that in winter his martens reduced their activity levels so as to save energy and minimise heat loss: in the coldest spells when the temperature fell to minus 20 °C a Białowieża pine marten was active on average for only two hours per night and travelled only 0.5 kilometres; this compared with an average of 13 active hours and 16 kilometres travelled per night in the balmy, prey-rich mid-summer period.

Recognising that male and female pine martens differ in size (males in Białowieża were 1.42 times heavier than females – this is called sexual dimorphism) and behaviour – mainly linked to their different roles in reproduction – yet have overlapping territories, Zalewski was able to explore his Białowieża dietary data for any differences in feeding ecology that might enable them to reduce competition for resources. During radio-tracking in the 1990s he was able to gather 697 scats from eight male martens and 506 scats from eight females. Analysis of the contents of these scats revealed some significant gender-related differences in the consumption of the main prey groups, and some of these differences were apparently influenced by variations in the abundance of small rodents – the main prey overall for both genders – and by seasonal factors. Thus, male martens ate more reptiles and amphibians than did females, which ate more squirrels than the males did (perhaps because the lighter females can pursue squirrels to places inaccessible to the heftier males?); males ate fewer small rodents than did the females in summer, autumn and winter, but more in spring; conversely, males ate more invertebrates in summer than did females.

The influence of rodent abundance was curiously complicated: for example, when rodent numbers were moderate to high, female martens ate more birds than did the males; while males ate more birds when rodent abundance was low; males tended to scavenge from ungulate carcasses more than the females did, although when rodent abundance was low females fed at carcasses to a similar degree; and males generally ate more fruit and fungi then the females did in high to moderate rodent years, although this situation was reversed in years of low rodent abundance.

The predator-prey arms race
A separate study of roost site selection by bats in Białowieża Forest reminds us that prey species are engaged in an enduring strategic battle to limit the impact of pine marten predation. Researchers from the Polish

Academy of Sciences radio-tracked noctule and Leisler's bats and found that, despite a very wide range of tree cavity shapes and sizes, both bat species selected roost sites in cavities with particular characteristics that reduced the risk of pine marten predation: firstly, the bats chose to roost in cavities that were on average at least 10 metres higher up trees than the average height of available cavities, so they were likely to be visited less frequently by a foraging marten than lower cavities; secondly, the bats avoided roosting in cavities with large entrances, so most roosts were in cavities with entrances narrower than the width of a pine marten's head (about 4.5–5 centimetres across); and finally, the cavities occupied by bats had a large internal 'marten distance', which means there was space for bats to roost inside the cavity well away from the entrance and out of reach of a hungry marten's raking, claw-tipped forelimbs.

So, despite one of their foraging strategies involving the agile exploration of elevated tree cavities upon which prey species are dependent for resting and breeding, pine martens do not have it easy because of the cunning choice of cavities by their potential prey. This is but one example of the arms race that defines the subtly shifting relationship between predators and their prey and which, in most cases, limits the impact of predation to sustainable levels.

Continental variations in feeding ecology

Having studied the feeding ecology of his Białowieża pine martens, Zalewski set about improving our understanding of large-scale geographical variations in the pine marten's food habits by reviewing the findings of published studies from across the species' range (but excluding Britain and Ireland, so continental studies only). This impressive effort drew upon the findings of 43 winter and 23 summer pine marten diet studies at a wide scatter of sites from Russia in the east across to Spain in the west; and from the Mediterranean islands of Mallorca and Menorca in the south up to Finland in the north. Zalewski looked especially for latitudinal variations in diet composition, as well as in the martens' food niche breadth (how diverse or narrow their diets were) and the size of prey consumed.

Considering all these continental studies together, small mammals (those weighing less than 150 grams) dominated the pine marten's diet during both summer (average 42 per cent of prey occurrences) and winter (47 per cent). Small mammals were followed in global importance by plant material (mainly fruit but including fungi – 21 per cent in summer, 16 per cent in winter), birds (13 per cent in summer, 15 per cent in winter), invertebrates (15 per cent in summer, 5 per cent in winter), medium-sized

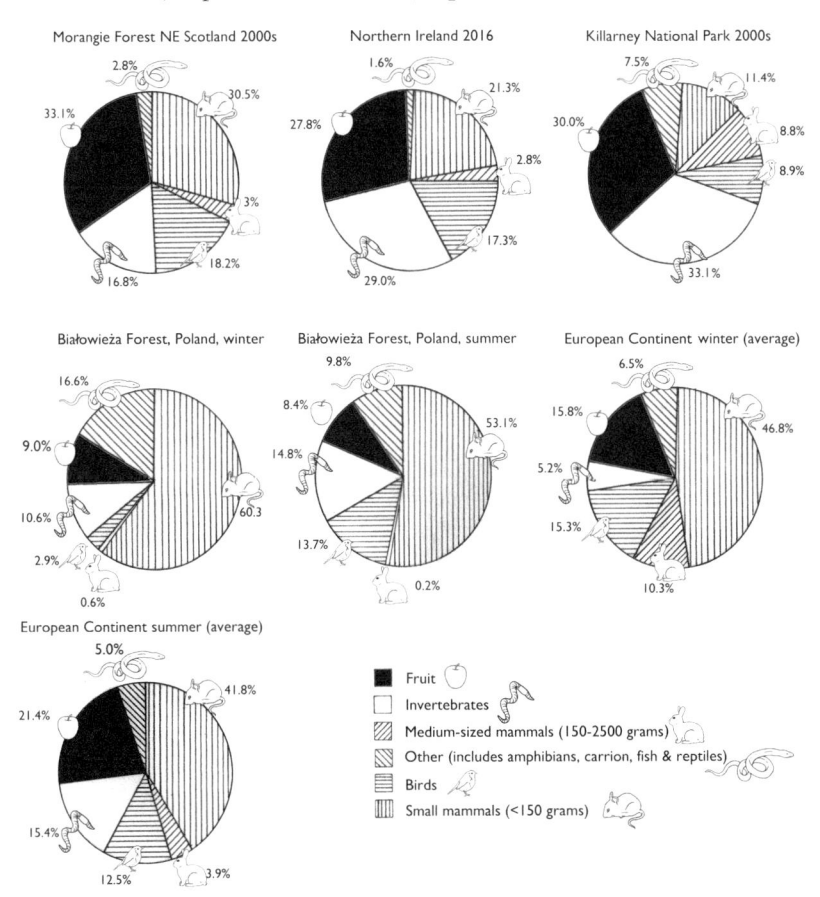

A summary of pine marten diets from Ireland, Scotland and eastern Poland, showing variations in the percentage occurrence of the main food categories (note the greater consumption of fruit and invertebrates in the western studies); also shown are the combined summer and winter diets from many studies across continental Europe, summarised by Andrzej Zalewski.

mammals (150–2,500 grams – 4 per cent in summer, 10 per cent in winter) and other material (including amphibians, carrion, fish and reptiles – 5 per cent in summer and 6 per cent in winter). There were some significant seasonal differences in the occurrence of these main categories in the pine marten's diet: medium-sized mammals were consumed significantly more in winter than in summer; and conversely plant materials (fruit and fungi) and invertebrates were both consumed more in summer than in winter.

One of the surprises to emerge from all these dietary studies – especially for those people who mistakenly view the pine marten as an arboreal species that spends much of its time up in the trees – is just how much of its food must be gathered or captured at or close to ground level: notably, the dominance of small mammals must mean that pine martens spend much of their time foraging on the woodland floor where – with some exceptions – most small mammals spend most of their time. Also striking is the breadth of the pine marten's foraging behaviour: from bilberries and beetles to the carcasses of wolf-killed deer, from honey to hares and from bank voles to black grouse, this is the diet of a true omnivore.

In terms of geographical patterns, Zalewski's review revealed striking contrasts between the winter diet of pine martens in the warm and dry south of Europe, where fruit was the dominant component, and the cooler north where pine martens ate a wider range of prey including more medium-sized mammals and birds. In the temperate zone in between these extremes small mammals were the dominant component. The pine marten's food niche breadth, the measure of dietary diversity, increased from south to north; and pine martens in the cold northern boreal zone also tended to consume the largest prey. Because larger prey items, such as squirrels, hares and grouse, are scarcer than small food such as voles and fruit, northern pine martens tended to travel greater distances when foraging than did the more frugivorous southern martens (8.1 kilometres per day at 70° North, compared with 2.5 kilometres per day at 40° North).

Curiously, Zalewski found that there was an inverse geographical relationship between the size of prey consumed and pine marten body size, so that pine martens in the north were smaller but ate larger prey than their larger southern relatives. This means that pine martens do not follow Bergman's rule, which predicts that a species' body size tends to increase from the south to the north of its range, where a lower surface area to volume ratio is an adaptation to colder conditions. Zalewski suggests that pine martens have opted for a different approach: smaller bodies mean lower energy requirements so, by successfully hunting larger prey in the colder north, pine martens can spend longer resting inside insulated den sites as a means to reduce energy loss.

Rodents rule
Given the importance of rodents in the pine marten's diet across its continental range, Zalewski looked into the particular species selected in different areas and how they might influence the performance of marten populations. He found that mice of the genus Apodemus (which includes our wood mouse and yellow-necked mouse) were most popular (on average 53 per cent of rodents consumed) in the Mediterranean region in the south of the marten's range, with their occurrence declining towards the north; further north in the temperate and boreal zones voles of the Myodes genus (related to our bank vole) were dominant at 46–52 per cent of rodents consumed, with Microtus voles representing 27–39 per cent; and in the far north lemmings were also eaten by pine martens.

Having demonstrated a numerical relationship between rodents and pine martens through his earlier Białowieża Forest study (see above), Zalewski found widespread evidence in other studies of a functional response in pine martens to fluctuations in the abundance of woodland rodents: this simply means that the proportion of rodents within pine marten diets is correlated with rodent abundance determined by trapping data; the relationship was especially strong in deciduous woodlands in the temperate zone, where forest rodents have high population densities and, unsurprisingly, pine marten diets are heavily dominated by rodents; and the species apparently driving this relationship were the Myodes voles, with no clear link shown with the other commonly consumed rodents of the genera Apodemus and Microtus. The clear continental preference among pine martens for Myodes voles is best explained by their similar habitat preferences – both favour woodlands – but then so do the wood mice and yellow-necked mice in the Apodemus genus. So perhaps bank voles are simply tastier than the other rodents; or are the mice just better at evading capture than the bank voles? If only we could speak martenese we could interview the consumers and answer these crucial questions!

Pine marten diets in Britain and Ireland

So, against the rich continental backdrop described above, what might be on the menu for pine martens at the wet and windy western edge of their global range? Among the modest number of published studies of pine marten feeding ecology in Britain and Ireland, the Scottish one by Fiona Caryl is probably the most elegant and detailed. In Britain, we are reliant on Scottish studies because, south of the border, pine martens are too rare for anyone to have studied their diets (although this should change soon following the VWT's successful translocation of pine martens to Wales). Through monthly collections in 2006 and 2007, Caryl and her team gathered an impressive 2,755 marten scats from her study site in and around Morangie Forest, just uphill of a famous whisky distillery (so that's why it tastes so special!).

Most of the Morangie scats were genetically confirmed as coming out of pine marten bottoms, and these 'dead cert' ones were used for identification of their contents, so we can have greater confidence in the findings of Caryl's study compared with less genetically rigorous ones. The Morangie martens' diet was dominated by three main food groups: small mammals (41 per cent), fruit (30 per cent) and birds (25 per cent). Despite these broad categories, over 90 per cent of the martens' food intake comprised just a few items. In striking contrast with continental studies, field voles comprised 40 per cent of the Morangie diet, with other small mammals making only tiny contributions despite the abundance of bank voles and wood mice in the study area. The fruit component was made up almost entirely of rowan berries and bilberries; and nearly all the birds were from the 'small bird' category. Other food items that were important in some continental studies, such as invertebrates and large mammals (mostly carrion), each comprised less than 2 per cent of the diet; and amphibians and reptiles were eaten infrequently. Though present in the study area, no red squirrels were recorded in the pine martens' diet.

Caryl's monthly scat collections revealed some marked variations in food intake across the year, with small mammals dominant in winter and spring and fruit top of the list in the autumn; only in the summer did the martens eat roughly equal proportions of small mammals, fruit and birds.

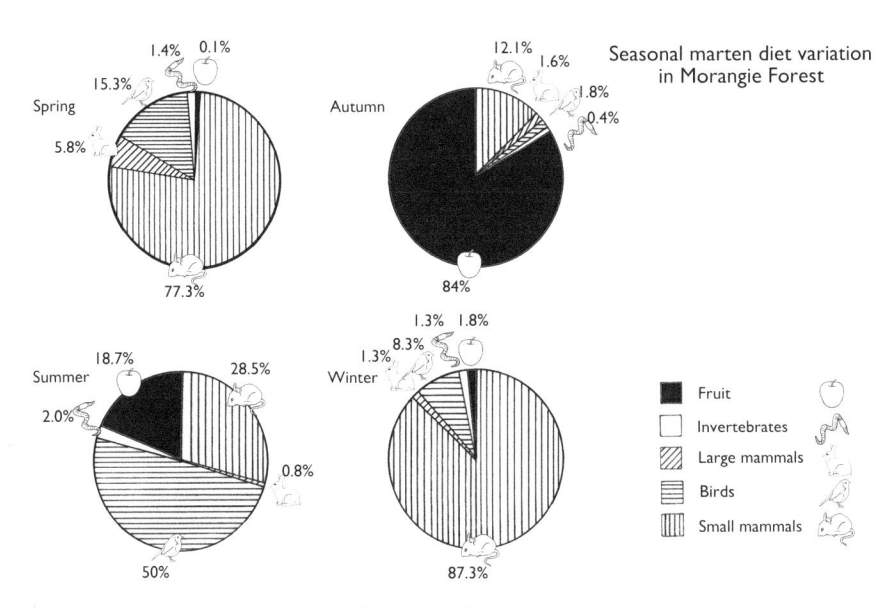

PINE MARTENS | FORAGING AND FOOD

Seasonal marten diet variation in Morangie Forest

Spring: 1.4%, 0.1%, 15.3%, 5.8%, 77.3%

Autumn: 12.1%, 1.6%, 1.8%, 0.4%, 84%

Summer: 18.7%, 28.5%, 2.0%, 0.8%, 50%

Winter: 1.3%, 1.8%, 8.3%, 1.3%, 87.3%

Legend:
- Fruit
- Invertebrates
- Large mammals
- Birds
- Small mammals

The study of pine marten feeding ecology in Morangie Forest in north-east Scotland, by Fiona Caryl, revealed the striking changes across the four seasons, with small mammals, birds and fruit taking turns to dominate the diet.

Why do Scottish pine martens prefer field voles?

In the field of Scottish pine marten ecology, one of the great mysteries is why most dietary studies have confirmed that pine martens prefer the humble field vole over all other small mammals, whereas in continental Europe it is the bank vole that is preferred. Could it be a function of habitat differences, with fragmented Scottish woodlands providing greater marten access to tussocky field vole habitat than in the more extensive continental forests? Or is it simply a matter of taste? Long, long ago, before the invention of Health and Safety, one brave man set out to answer this crucial question by comparing the taste of different small mammals as part of his own study of pine marten diet in Scotland: Rob Coope found that voles did indeed taste and smell better than mice or shrews (shrews tasted worst of all); but he could not distinguish between the taste of field and bank voles, so the question remains essentially unresolved.

My introduction to the 'differentness' of Irish martens started when I visited Dromore Wood in County Clare, where Paddy O'Sullivan had studied pine martens in the late 1970s and revealed the surprisingly high population that it supported. Many of the marten scats we found there on a lovely spring day were full of the blackish remains of ivy berries – for ivy is one of the few wild plants to produce its fruit so early in the year.

More recent studies confirm the greater frugivorous and insectivorous tendencies of Irish pine martens compared with other studies in which mammal prey tends to dominate. Firstly, in the early 2000s, Áine Lynch and Yvonne McCann collected and analysed 387 pine marten scats from Killarney National Park in the south-west of Ireland (see table below). Even though Killarney lies within the expanding range of the introduced bank vole in Ireland, small mammals comprise a small proportion of the total diet, which is dominated by fruit and (at least numerically – see table) invertebrates. Amongst the wide range of fruits consumed, ivy berries were by far the most important, with yew berries in second place.

The Lynch and McCann study reveals an important caveat when assessing the contribution of small, easily recognisable items like beetles: they presented their data in three ways – as percentage frequency occurrence (the commonest way of describing carnivore diets), percentage mass in scats and percentage fresh weight ingested (this last one involves the application of a simple correction factor for each food type); this showed that, although arthropods may be numerically abundant in scats, their actual contribution to the diet is much smaller when their limited bulk is taken into account. Conversely, because fruit tends to be easily digestible and so leaves rather few remains in scats, the conversion factor elevates its total contribution from 30 per cent frequency occurrence to over half of the fresh weight of food ingested.

	% Frequency occurrence	% Mass in scats	% Fresh weight ingested
Beetles	22.99	4.19	1.61
Bees/wasps	0.79	0.16	0.06
Butterflies/moths	0.68	0.06	0.05
Wood-lice	0.91	0.06	0.02
Larvae	0.11	0.03	0.01
Not identified	3.74	0.56	0.22
Total Arthropods	**29.22**	**5.07**	**1.97**

	% Frequency occurrence	% Mass in scats	% Fresh weight ingested
Blackberry	2.26	2.92	0.03
Bilberry	1.47	2.08	2.23
Ivy	16.65	26.18	28.12
Rowan	0.91	0.3	0.3
Yew	6.12	15.65	16.8
Apple	0.57	0.14	0.15
Hawthorn	0.11	0.09	0.09
Pine	0.45	0.03	0.03
Not identified	1.47	0.56	0.6
Total Fruit	**30.01**	**47.95**	**51.44**
Woodmouse	5.77	4.44	7.49
Bank vole	4.42	3.85	6.49
Pygmy shrew	1.24	0.99	0.02
Common rat	0.11	0.43	1.41
Red squirrel	0.45	0.07	0.12
Rabbit or hare	0.45	0.18	0.3
Deer	0.23	0.09	0.43
Not identified	7.59	5.24	8.85
Total Mammals	**20.27**	**15.29**	**26.73**
Song birds	3.17	1.02	2.89
Falcons	0.11	0.29	0.83
Egg shell	0.34	0.008	0.001
Not identified	5.32	3.14	8.94
Total Birds	**8.95**	**4.47**	**12.66**
Snail	0.9	0.03	0.037
Common frog	5.44	3.89	5.38
Debris	2.15	1.49	0.11
Total Other	**8.49**	**5.42**	**5.41**
Earthworm (chaetae)	3.05	-	1.67

The diet of pine martens in the broadleaf woodlands of Killarney National Park, south-west Ireland between 2003 and 2005, based on analysis of 387 scats by Áine Lynch and Yvonne McCann. (Data as presented in Lynch and McCann, 2007, Proceedings of the Royal Irish Academy, vol. 107B, no. 2, 67–76)

For comparison with Lynch and McCann's study in the south-west of Ireland, PhD student Josh Twining has generously made available some preliminary results from his 2016/2017 study of pine marten diet across 28 sites in Northern Ireland. His analysis of a 399 scat subset of more than a thousand scats reveals that invertebrates comprised some 29 per cent (frequency occurrence) of the diet year-round, with beetles the dominant component (24 per cent) and a smattering of other creepy-crawlies such as bees (probably ingested by martens in pursuit of honey), slugs, snails and earthworms. Fruit comprised 28 per cent frequency occurrence – albeit consumption was seasonally concentrated – with rowan, blackberry, bilberry and hawthorn the main contributors in order of importance. Despite the impoverished small mammal fauna, this group contributed 21 per cent in Twining's study, with pygmy shrew and wood mouse the key species; larger mammals were of minor significance at 3 per cent and comprised the carrion of sheep and deer and the occasional lagomorph (rabbits and hares). Birds contributed some 17 per cent, with Passeriformes (perching birds) the dominant group and consumption concentrated in the spring and summer. Finally, miscellaneous items such as common frog, human refuse and unidentified items made up about 2 per cent.

Although at this stage in Twining's dietary analysis only per cent frequency occurrence information was available, his findings in Northern Ireland appear broadly similar to those from the far south-west of Ireland, albeit with a slightly higher consumption of small mammals and birds apparent in the north. Both studies confirm the special importance of fruit and insects compared with most other studies in the pine marten's range. In that respect, Irish pine martens seem to have a feeding ecology more like that of the mainly frugivorous and insectivorous stone marten elsewhere in Europe.

Caching of food
When pine martens have caught or gathered more food than they can eat, it is common for them to cache it somewhere safe for later consumption. Usually it involves relatively large prey items, such as a pigeon or grey squirrel, rather than small stuff like voles or fruit. Typically, they choose sheltered places well above ground level so that neither the weather nor

other predators can spoil their chance of a future feast; so, tree cavities, large bird boxes or the rafters of barns and outhouses may end up as pine marten larders. However, these carefully stored meals are not always eaten by their owners: on Morvern in the West of Scotland, Matt Wilson noticed the remains of a bird stuffed above a rafter high up in his shed; on reaching up to identify it – a hooded crow – he was rewarded with a facial shower of maggots falling from the rotting carcass!

MARTEN COMMUNICATIONS

Scented messages
Although pine martens live most of their lives in separate territories, communication between individuals plays a crucial role in the defence of those territories and the resources they hold, in ensuring that adult males and females meet during the mating season, and in enabling mothers to rear their kits successfully to independence. In common with many other solitary mammals – and especially those that occupy cluttered environments through which sound doesn't travel well – much of the communication between pine martens is scent-based, with scent produced from glands inside the anus, on the abdomen, feet and possibly elsewhere. In common with other Carnivores martens also use urine in scent-based communication. However, to we humans, scats play the most visible part in the exchange of scented messages between martens. A pair of scent glands just inside the anus ensure that, as each scat is produced, it is coated in a veneer of mucus that holds and emits a scent unique to the animal that produced it. I have written above at great length (perhaps too much for some?) about marten scats, where they are deposited and how wonderful they smell.

The need to defend resources and find a partner during the mating season can be stressful, and this is reflected in patterns of scat deposition by pine martens. A study in north-western Spain by Isabel Barja and colleagues measured levels of the physiological stress hormone cortisol in scats left by wild pine martens. They found that, for both males and females, scats deposited in conspicuous locations – so presumably intended for communication – had higher mean cortisol levels than did those deposited in inconspicuous places. So, anxious martens are more likely to poo flamboyantly to ensure that others get the message, while relaxed martens are content to poo in private!

By depositing scats strategically in places where other martens will find them, such as on elevated objects and on tracks and paths through woodland, a pine marten can use its waste material to deliver scented messages that communicate the same types of information that we humans achieve via 'KEEP OUT' notices and dating websites. But scats are simply the visible component of scent-based communication; there is

A study led by Isobel Barja revealed higher levels of stress hormones in pine marten scats deposited in conspicuous places for social communication purposes.

much more scented marten chatter that we humans cannot hope to tune in to!

Recent use of camera traps to film pine martens, as well as observations of captive animals, has revealed the extent of scent-marking behaviour that does not involve scats. Video evidence shows that, as when defaecating, pine martens sometimes do a 'hip wiggle' when urinating to produce a wavy dribble of wee. However, most scent comes from the abdominal and anal scent glands, which produce scented unguents that are variously daubed, smeared, wiped and rubbed on to suitable objects (including other martens) within their environment. People who watch pine martens at feeding stations and on camera trap video footage will notice that they frequently rub their bums, bellies and chests over all sorts of objects to leave scented messages. Captive pine martens are reported to have favourite 'rubbing places' where they repeatedly lie down to rub their undersides, such as on the lids of their den boxes or particular tree branches within their cages.

The abdominal gland is most obvious in adult males as a waxy, bald patch just in front of the penis tuft on the animal's underside between the belly and chest. David Balharry measured the size of these bald areas in pine martens that he live-trapped in Scotland's north-west Highlands; he found they were biggest in males over three years old with higher testosterone levels – these dominant, older males are much more active during the mating season than lower status younger males; and there was a seasonal pattern, with the bald patch area peaking in older males at around 800 square millimetres in June and July before declining to less than 300 square millimetres over winter. This pattern suggests that the abdominal glands must play a part in scent-based communication during the pine marten mating season.

As well as coating faeces with scented mucus, the anal glands can be used in the absence of faecal matter to 'set scent': this involves a marten pressing its anus on to an object or rubbing it along the ground or a fallen log to leave a personal smear of scent from the anal glands. Martens that are on friendly terms sometimes mark each other with a quick press of their anal scent glands, rather like a clan of badgers that build up a 'group niff' through mutual scent-marking.

Yo GIRLS! CHECK MY GLAND OUT!

Although most scent-marking involves a single marten depositing scent on its own to leave messages for other martens and, perhaps, to spread a reassuring personal whiff around a resident's territory, there is evidence that marking may facilitate social interactions between adults during the mating season. A study of captive American martens (closely related to our pine marten) by Joel Heath and colleagues revealed a strong link between scent-marking and interactions between a male and a receptive female, and suggested a major female influence on male marking and activity. An increase in scent marking has also been reported in captive British pine martens during the mating season, especially involving the abdominal scent glands, with much belly-rubbing between bouts of sexual activity.

Vocalisations

Pine martens produce a surprising variety of noises that play a part in close-quarters social contact – both aggressive and friendly – as well as courtship and mating activity, family life and interactions with other species. The variety of sounds suggests that pine martens enjoy more of a social life than we normally associate with a solitary mustelid. My only direct experience of pine marten noises in the wild are the low, threatening growl from an adult when one approaches its den too closely, and the gentle, plaintiff squeaks of young kits when their mother is disturbed in a natal den. But there is a growing catalogue of descriptions and recordings made by others of pine marten noises, starting with the late naturalist H. G. Hurrell, who wrote about his captive and free-ranging martens in Devon in the mid-twentieth century. Many of the descriptions below are taken from his observations.

The use of camera traps that record sound has recently added to our knowledge of noisy interactions between martens at feeding stations, where aggressive interactions are common. I have seen video footage of one marten chasing another off a feeding station with a harsh blast of screeching and chattering. Other cross sounds during encounters between adults are described by H. G. Hurrell as huffing, grunting and high-pitched squealing and snarling, uttered with 'antagonistic vehemence'. Aggressive noises are also heard at den sites where one marten invades the personal space of another: in the Scottish Highlands, David Balharry heard snarling when one radio-tagged female approached the den of another; and again when an adult male approached the breeding den of a female and she 'saw him off' with a bout of snarling before he got too close. Pine martens may also give a short, sharp warning bark when surprised by humans.

I learnt more about marten noises while helping the VWT to transport wild-caught Scottish animals to Wales as part of their recovery project. Most martens in cage traps remained quiet, but sometimes a particularly feisty captive would give vent to a throaty, grunty/buzzy snarling noise that subsided into bouts of harrumphing as it calmed down again. On the long car journey south, although appearing remarkably calm most of the time in their cosy, hay-filled cages, the pine martens occasionally made gentle puffing/panting heh-heh-heh noises.

It is during courtship and copulation that 'marten music' is at its sweetest and most diverse, with much chittering, clucking, purring and friendly growling. A female in oestrus is reported to make excited, high-pitched clucking sounds, believed to attract males; and during copulation both animals vocalise non-aggressively for extended periods – for each mating bout may last for an hour or more – with the male tending to emit a quiet, low-pitched growling (sometimes also made by the female), while the female makes higher-pitched clucking and purring noises (males can purr as well).

Ten months after the 'marten music' of copulation, some adult female martens find themselves rearing kits and a new set of sounds are involved in the cut and thrust of family life. The young kits express their needs through high-pitched mewing and squeaking and, when older, may call for their mother with a harsh yowling-screech that has been likened to the sound of tearing paper. The mother tries to keep her kits in order with a reassuring clucking, chuntering or purring sound. When a mother marten is more stressed, such as when she perceives that one of her kits is being threatened by a human, she may chitter aggressively.

Tail-swishing

H. G. Hurrell described an agitated marten grunting emphatically while making vigorous side-to-side movements of its tail. At his wildlife hides in Scotland, James Moore has twice recorded cat-like 'tail-swishing' by a pine marten that appeared to be directed aggressively at another marten at a feeding station; he has also recorded a marten tail-swishing at a badger in a similar situation; and at his feeding station on the Black Isle

James Hislop has observed tail-swishing in martens that were apparently alert and listening out for foxes or other martens. As in domestic cats, tail-swishing seems to be a sign of irritation or vigilant grumpiness in martens in certain social situations.

Tail-swishing may be used as a visible threat to other martens or other species nearby and perhaps to signal dominance – though it seems unlikely that a badger would feel intimidated by it. Pine martens also use tail-swishing when bothered by people who approach a den: Colin Leslie has observed this at marten dens in the Scottish Highlands, when an adult marten typically growls and tail-swishes from a high branch at a person down below. Because pine martens have such large tails it would make sense to use them as warning signals of grumpiness in close-quarters interactions with other martens, or as a warning to other species that might pose a threat, rather as squirrels do.

MATING AND BREEDING

Breeding slow but long

Pine martens are very slow breeders, mainly because they produce only small litters – typically just two or three kits, and this has a profound influence upon their population biology. It limits the capacity of populations to grow when conditions improve, so population recovery and range expansion take a long time as we have seen in Scotland; and it makes populations vulnerable to a slight increase in mortality levels, so elevated rates of predation or culling can drive a population down or bring recovery to a grinding halt.

As well as producing small litters, pine martens are slow to start breeding, and this adds to the vulnerability of populations: in David Balharry's study in the Scottish Highlands all males under three years of age were classed as non-breeding (see *The male 'teenage' phase*, page 130); similarly, young females normally do not give birth before the age of two years. This means that young martens of both genders have to establish a good territory and survive unscathed for two or three years before they can start to contribute to population growth, something that cannot be taken for granted wherever foxes or lethal traps are abundant.

In comparison, weasels and stoats are very fast out of the reproductive starting blocks (stoats indecently so): female weasels become sexually mature at three to four months so are capable of breeding in their first year, and adult females can produce two litters of up to eight kits each in a single year; stoats produce even larger litters (up to 13) in which the female kits are sexually mature before their eyes open; so adult males can copulate with mothers and daughters in one fell swoop, ensuring that the latter are pregnant before they leave the natal den. This makes stoats very effective colonists, with each young female fully loaded to found a new population before she disperses; and the high reproductive potential of both stoats and weasels enables populations to persist in the face of high mortality, and to respond quickly when conditions improve. This is one reason why these smaller mustelids remained relatively common and widespread during the Victorian era of heaviest game-keeping pressure that drove polecats and pine martens so close to extinction in Britain.

On the other side of the coin, pine martens are capable of living longer than most other British and Irish mustelids, so the potential lifetime productivity of each breeding female marten is comparable with the other species. But, as with the young pre-breeding martens, much depends upon each breeding female maintaining a territory in which premature mortality can be avoided.

The mating season

Adult female pine martens embark upon an oestrus cycle in mid-summer once their maternal duties are reduced because their kits have achieved semi-independence; this cycle involves bouts of 1–4 days of sexual receptivity separated by gaps of 6–17 days; the only external evidence of oestrus (though you have to get pretty close to notice it) is a swelling of the vulva, which also changes colour. So, in mid-summer adult males range widely in search of oestrus females, and scent marking activity reaches a peak as martens leave their saucy scented messages to facilitate contact (so it is a good time to undertake scat surveys).

When two adults meet and engage in courtship, there is much playful chasing and lots of noise made by both participants (see *Vocalisations*, page 120). Mating may start with the male gripping the female by the scruff of the neck to restrain her, and there may be displays of physical dominance as he drags her about by the neck prior to mating, but in pine martens there is less reliance on brute force than in other small mustelids: two camera trap images of mating martens taken by James Bunyan on 4 July 2014 in the Scottish Highlands show the female standing compliantly during copulation, with the male not biting her neck in either photograph (in one of them he appears to be grinning sheepishly at the camera). This more cooperative approach to copulation explains why recently mated female martens do not show the severe neck injuries – called mating scars – typically found in female mink and polecats.

Most matings occur in July or August, but some occur a bit earlier when dependent kits are still with their mothers: I saw video footage, taken in June 2015, of an adult male marten invading a natal den in the west of Scotland to mate with a breeding female in full view of her well-grown but still dependent kits aged eight or nine weeks; and in captivity matings have been observed into early September. Mating in pine martens is promiscuous, with each gender willing to mate with several individuals of the opposite sex; as a consequence, male martens play no part in rearing young because they are very likely to have been fathered by a rival male; so the entire job of rearing kits is left to the females.

Delayed implantation and gestation

After the summer mating season, there is an extended period of about 230 days before the blastocysts implant and gestation begins early in the following year. The timing of implantation ranges between mid-January and mid-March across the pine marten's range; the local timing is believed to be influenced by changing day length; and the number of blastocysts implanting may be influenced by food availability (which, in turn, determines the physical condition of the adult female – see Mast and mice control the martens, below). The post-implantation gestation period is 30 days. Pregnant martens usually select the structure in which they will give birth – known as the natal den – in February or March, although one of 'our' females in Galloway Forest didn't move into her natal den box until 1 April and gave birth a few days later.

Birth dates and litter sizes

Most young pine martens are born between mid-March and mid-April; in Scotland, we occasionally hear of kits born at the end of February; and in the Netherlands litters exceptionally arrive in the first week of May. This spread is not simply due to regional variations within the pine marten's huge Eurasian range, for even within the same locality births may be spread over three weeks: in Galloway Forest in 2017 estimated litter birth dates ranged from 1 to 23 April; and in wild pine martens in the Netherlands between 2008 and 2014 Hans Kleef and Henri Wijsman recorded mean annual birth dates between 5 and 14 April, with a peak in the second week of April.

Pine marten litter sizes are small when compared with most other mustelids: the average across Western Europe is 2.7, with the range typically from one to five. Higher figures from Russia in the early 1980s – average 3.5 with a range of one to eight – feels like cold war propaganda. In Scotland, it is unusual to hear of litters of more than three kits; and in our Galloway study the norm is two kits. In the Netherlands, average litter sizes varied between 2.43 and 2.98 over a ten-year period from 2005. Some of these estimates are derived around weaning time, so may not take account of pre-weaning mortality; Dan Farrow at the Wildwood Trust in Kent reports that their captive pine martens normally produce 1–3 kits, with only one litter of four recorded.

Mast and mice control the martens

We know that pine martens show a numerical response to fluctuations in their rodent prey. The mechanics of this link have been revealed by a recent study of pine marten reproduction in two areas in the Netherlands. Kleef and Wijsman recorded litter sizes and birth dates in 372 wild-born litters between 2005 and 2014; they also recorded beech and oak mast production and wood mouse abundance in the same forests. Kleef and Wijsman found that wood mouse numbers were especially high after good mast years, and in turn mouse abundance influenced pine marten breeding success, with larger litters in 'high' wood mouse years; notably, unusually large litters of four or five kits mainly occurred in years of peak wood mouse

> abundance. This study revealed that wood mouse abundance also affected marten birth dates and the foraging activity of mothers: kits were born on average a week earlier in peak wood mouse years than in 'low' mouse years; and mother martens foraged on average for an hour longer each day in years of low wood mouse abundance compared with 'high' mouse years.

Development of kits

Baby pine martens are usually called kits and are born about the size of a man's index finger and weighing about 30 grams, with eyes and ears closed and the body covered in fine, sparse silvery grey hairs. At this stage, in order to maintain their body temperature, kits are heavily dependent upon their mother's body heat and the insulative properties of the natal den in which she produced them. Natal dens in tree cavities typically have a cosy basal layer of soft woody debris and frass (the dung of wood-boring insects) into which the kits can nestle, especially when their mother makes her brief excursions for food and water.

Apart from a graph of increasing bodyweight against age in captive pine marten kits, produced by Dr Fritz Schmidt in 1943, there is no published information on the pattern of kit growth. However, Hans Kleef has gathered valuable evidence from wild-born litters in the Netherlands, and this reveals considerable variation in the link between kit age and bodyweight, as we have also found in Galloway Forest.

By about three weeks of age the kits' sparse silvery grey hairs have been replaced by a dense, soft, woolly brown fur over most of the body; the pale chest patch is now visible and the ears are more prominent and have a fringe of pale fur. Also noticeable is a large cluster of whitish guard hairs centred on the nape of the neck. I suggest this pale nape patch, which is no longer present when marten kits first emerge from the natal den at the age of seven to eight weeks, is a helpful target for a mother marten in the murky confines of the natal den, enabling her to pinpoint the safest place to grip with her teeth in order to rescue a kit from danger. This visible pale target is especially valuable if kits fall out of an elevated natal den on to the dark woodland floor, as they sometimes do when they become more mobile and start to explore.

A series of video clips – known as the Pine Marten Diaries and shared on Facebook during 2016 and 2017 – taken from inside a den box used by a wild breeding female in the West of Scotland have revealed much about pine marten family life before the kits emerge from the natal den. Occasionally a mother marten moves her kits between den sites when they are less than three weeks old, but most mothers stay put with their litters until they are weaned. When a mother returns to the den after a foraging trip her first activity is to lick the kits' abdomens to stimulate their passage of urine and faeces – you can hear her slurping and guzzling as she consumes the material. Despite their mother's reassuring chuntering, the kits sometimes screech and squeal as they resent being woken suddenly for a vigorous licking of their private parts.

When the kits are newly born, mother martens make only brief excursions out of the natal den, totalling about two hours per day according to a study by Kleef and Wijsman in the Netherlands. However, the total duration of maternal foraging bouts increases steeply during the 45-day lactation period to 6–8 hours per day when the kits are 5–6 weeks old. The kits' eyes open at 35 days and weaning starts soon afterwards – usually in mid-May in Scotland – and mothers bring items of prey back to the natal den for their kits to chew on.

Conveniently for hard-pressed mother martens, the weaning process coincides with the time when other mothers are busy producing vulnerable, bite-sized babies of their own: for example, fledgling birds are abundantly available as marten food in mid-May if the right habitat occurs within commuting distance of natal dens. At this time of year, it is not unusual to find a few prey items, such as mice, voles and small birds, stored in the entrances of natal den boxes or hanging on nearby branches or on the ground beneath. But on 21 May 2015 in Galloway Forest, we encountered an extraordinary case of maternal over-supply at a den box containing two kits: one of the box entrances was stuffed with fresh prey; the box lid was similarly piled high and the forest floor beneath was littered with further items that had fallen from the box. We counted 53 fresh prey items comprising 44 fledgling birds (mostly robins, chaffinches, wrens and tits), two field voles, three wood mice, three common shrews and a frog. This mother was clearly an unusually efficient hunter that could not adjust her effort to match her kits' appetites.

When we find pine marten kits in the den boxes in our Galloway Forest study – in mid-May when kits are three to six weeks old and weighing 300 to 600 grams – we have noticed patterns of behaviour that must be adaptations to being born in an elevated den with the associated risk of falling to the ground. Firstly, when we lift the lid of a den box, the young martens stay very still and appear calm, presumably because this is a safer response to danger than to rush about and risk falling to the ground; even when we briefly handle the kits they remain still and never struggle or attempt to bite us. When we hold the kits, we notice the surprising strength of their well-developed limbs and their instinct to grip anything within reach with their needle-sharp claws – this too must be an adaptation to reduce the risk of falling. When a marten kit does fall out of an elevated den in a tree hole or box – not unusual according to recent video evidence – the mother nips down the tree to retrieve it, carries it back up the trunk by gripping the scruff of its neck in her teeth, and shoves it unceremoniously back inside the den; but if she is away foraging when a kit falls it will be at risk of predation until she returns.

Natal den relocation
Beyond the very early movement of kits between dens reported above, the main period of den relocation occurs later. When pine marten kits start exploring the entrance to their natal den – usually in late May – they are very clumsy and lacking in confidence as arboreal climbers. Because the risk of kits falling to the ground increases at this critical stage in their development, mother martens typically respond by moving them to a new den that provides safer opportunities for learning to climb. For example, in the Netherlands, where pine martens commonly use woodpecker holes in smooth-barked beech trees as natal dens, mother martens tend to move their kits to a new den in a rough-barked tree such as an oak where they can gain confidence as climbers more safely.

There may be other reasons for marten families to relocate to a new den when the kits are becoming more mobile in late May: conditions in the natal den may have become too cramped and whiffy; there might have been an irritating build-up of ectoparasites; and local prey populations may have become depleted by the mother's concentrated foraging during the weaning period, meaning that a move to another part of her home range becomes necessary.

From late May onwards, young pine martens in commercial forests sometimes use stacks of timber as safe hiding or resting places in midsummer, something observed by forester Gareth Ventress. This is not a cause for concern until the time comes for timber to be sold and removed from the forest, so precautions are needed to avoid harm to any marten youngsters hiding in timber stacks.

Sub-adult pine martens reach adult body size when they are 6–8 months old, so by October to December in the year of their birth they become difficult to distinguish from adults, although experienced observers may spot them for their pristine fur, needle-sharp teeth and baby-faced, playful demeanour.

Young pine marten kits typically have a cluster of white hairs on the nape of the neck, perhaps to help their mother locate the safest place to grip them if she needs to move or rescue them.

Juvenile dispersal

Juvenile dispersal is the journey made by a young marten between its natal range and the place where it establishes its own home range, which may be several kilometres away. Young pine martens seem to disperse later than other mustelids, perhaps because of their extended sub-adult phase that encourages adult martens to tolerate their continued presence (see below). This explains why amicable groups of two or three pine martens are sometimes seen together in late winter and spring before or during dispersal. Exceptionally, family groups may stay together much later than this: Ruth Hanniffy of the VWT reported a case from County Cavan in Ireland where, in May 2017, a roof void was occupied by a mother marten and her new kits, together with her three full-grown offspring from the previous year. The human residents of the dwelling found it difficult to tolerate the rumpus they caused, so the VWT advised on a humane way to encourage the marten family to move on.

A study by Jérémy Larroque and colleagues at the University of Lyon and the Office National de la Chasse et de la Faune Sauvage revealed that in the Bresse Region of France young pine martens of both genders tended to disperse between mid-February and mid-March in the year following their birth, when they were about 11 months old. This timing coincides with the early stages of gestation in adult females, with associated hormonal changes making them extra grumpy about the idle presence of last year's progeny loitering around the home range and eating all the food. Larroque and co. noticed that the late winter dispersal period also coincided with a period of testis growth in sub-adult males, doubtless leading to teenage aggression as a further stimulus to dispersal. All those surging hormones probably mean that late winter is a socially stressful time in pine marten populations.

The male 'teenage' phase

In his study of pine martens in the Scottish Highlands in the late 1980s and early '90s, in which he was able to age the animals he live-trapped (by removing a tooth and counting the cementum rings), David Balharry found maturity-related differences in males either side of three years old: males over three years had large, active abdominal scent glands and showed seasonally elevated testosterone levels; males less than three years old showed neither of these things, so Balharry classed them as non-breeding animals. More recently, wildlife vet Alex Tomlinson, who examined many sedated male Scottish pine martens in her role in the VWT's Pine Marten Recovery Project, noted that young males tend to have smaller testes and bacula than older ones.

These observations support the view that male pine martens have an extended sub-adult stage in which maturity is delayed until they have passed their third birthdays. By postponing their sexual maturity and behaving like subordinates for a year or two, younger males may be tolerated by older martens and so avoid some of the aggression that might otherwise come their way. Also, this male 'teenage phase' seems a sensible reproductive strategy in animals that may live for approaching ten years in the wild. Why rush to sexual maturity in your second year only to get beaten up by older, more experienced males in the hectic hurly-burly of the mating season? Far better to bide your time and join the fray two years later when you have a much better chance of competing for access to receptive females.

Things are a bit different for young female pine martens because they reach sexual maturity in the year following their birth, so are likely to be mated first in their second summer when they are about 16 months old; but because of the long period of delayed implantation they do not first give birth until their own third birthdays.

Longevity
As in other carnivores, many martens die before they reach two years of age; nevertheless, their potential lifespan is longer than most other mustelids. Peter Stuart and Colin Lawton found that one third of Irish road casualty pine martens were aged 9–11 years, so this is indicative of their maximum life span, though animals in captivity can live until they are 20 or more. Excessive tooth wear leading to starvation is probably a major cause of death in animals that manage to avoid earlier and more violent fatalities. In Scotland, two out of 34 martens aged by Balharry were seven years old; and in the Bresse Region of France the oldest pine marten recorded by Ruette and colleagues in a lethally trapped population was eight years old.

HOW MANY MARTENS?

Improving abundance estimates

It has recently become easier to answer the typical journalist's question 'how many pine martens are there?' This is thanks to a series of studies that have produced reliable population density estimates based mainly on radio-tracking or non-invasive genotyping (collecting fresh scat or hair samples from which DNA analysis can identify individual martens). These estimates are shown in the table below; they reveal a similar pattern to that previously shown for home ranges, in which population densities tend to be greater in the higher quality habitats because individual martens occupy smaller home ranges so you can fit more of them in. There is one caveat, however, that may apply to certain forest habitats: in Declan O'Mahony's study in upland conifer plantations at Killavoggy he found that, although home ranges were relatively small, there were big gaps between some home ranges so the pine martens did not occupy the whole of the forest area upon which his population density estimate was based; O'Mahony suggests that this patchy occupancy may be a feature of commercial forests, where timber harvesting activities make some areas temporarily unattractive to pine martens.

Study area	Method	Population density (no. per square kilometre)	Lead author(s) and year of publication
Scotland			
Strathglass, Inverness-shire	Radio-tracking	0.42	D. Balharry 1993
Novar, Ross-shire	Radio-tracking	*0.58	E. Halliwell 1997
Glen Trool, Galloway Forest	Radio-tracking	*0.119–0.221	P. Bright and T. Smithson 1997
Minnoch, Galloway Forest	Radio-tracking	*0.030– 0.094	P. Bright and T. Smithson 1997
Fleet Basin, Galloway Forest	Non-invasive genotyping	*0.08	E. Croose 2015

Abernethy, Cairngorms National Park	Non-invasive genotyping	0.38	L. Kubasiewicz 2014
Mar Lodge, Cairngorms National Park	Non-invasive genotyping	0.07	L. Kubasiewicz 2014
Inshriach Forest, Cairngorms National Park	Non-invasive genotyping	0.18	L. Kubasiewicz 2014
Ireland			
Mourne Mountains, Northern Ireland	Non-invasive genotyping	*0.53	D. O'Mahony 2015
Kilavoggy, County Leitrim	Live-trapping and radio-tracking	*0.46	D. O'Mahony 2014
County Kerry	Non-invasive genotyping	0.5–2	A. Lynch 2006
County Wicklow	Non-invasive genotyping	1.01*	E. Sheehy 2013
County Waterford	Non-invasive genotyping	2	J. Mullins 2010
Counties Laois and Offaly	Non-invasive genotyping	3.13*	E. Sheehy 2013

*Pine marten population density estimates derived from radio-tracking and non-invasive genetic sampling. *Denotes density estimate for adults only.*

National population estimates

As well as these site-specific population density estimates, an ambitious government-backed plan was launched in the Republic of Ireland in 2016 to produce a Pine Marten Population Assessment (PMPA) for the whole country. Led by Declan O'Mahony, hair tube sampling in 14 randomly selected study sites was used to gather material for genotyping by the Gene-genies at Waterford Institute of Technology. Spatially explicit capture-recapture models were then used to produce population density estimates for each site; and extrapolation from these produced a population estimate of 3,043 pine martens for the Republic of Ireland. This is probably the largest ever study of pine marten population density in the world, covering many thousands of hectares of forest; it should help the Irish Government to respond sensibly to recent calls by one or two farmers for pine martens to be culled in order to protect sheep flocks.

In Britain, The Mammal Society has recently (2018) produced a pine marten population estimate as part of its review of the abundance and status of all British mammals. Drawing upon both existing survey information and expert opinion, the estimate for Britain (meaning Scotland, Wales and England) is 3,700 pine martens (with a range of 1,600 to 8,900 reflecting the relatively low reliability of the estimate). This represents only 2.5 per cent of the British marten population in the Mesolithic before we humans started making such a mess of things.

Tempting though it is to expect marten range expansion to continue on our islands, we have to acknowledge the severe constraints imposed by our still limited woodland cover, which remains one of the lowest in Europe: According to Teagasc, woodland cover in Eire is 11 per cent; comparable Forestry Commission data are 18 per cent in Scotland, 15 per cent in Wales and 10 per cent in England; the average over the whole of the UK (i.e. including Northern Ireland at 8 per cent) was just 13 per cent. For comparison, most of the rest of Europe is more than 30 per cent wooded (average 46 per cent), with the leaders Finland, Sweden and the Russian Federation respectively on 73, 68 and 50 per cent. So, if we want pine martens to thrive on our islands we need to see those magnificent 'Lawton Principles' – More, Bigger, Better (I would add 'Older') and Joined Up – applied to our woodland cover, with appropriate targets and incentives to turn intention into action.

The martens of Portlaw Woods, Eire

As an adjunct to their ground-breaking work on non-invasive field techniques, my Gene-genie friends Pete Turner and Catherine O'Reilly undertook a ten-year study of the pine martens living in Portlaw Woods in County Waterford between 2006 and 2015. Using a combination of hair tubes and scat surveys to gather DNA samples for genotyping, backed up by occasional live-trapping, they identified all the pine martens present each year in the 330 hectare woodland. The number of adult territory-holders resident at any one time ranged between four and six, representing a relatively high adult population density of 1.2 to 1.8 martens per square kilometre. However, taking account of kits, pre-dispersal juveniles and occasional immigrants, the total number of martens present ranged between nine and 22, representing a maximum density of 2.7 to 6.7 per square kilometre. Through their long-term study of resident martens, Turner and O'Reilly were able to observe the way that individual territories changed in size and shape from year to year in response to the disappearance of or pressure from neighbouring territory-holders. Nevertheless, most territory-holders stayed put for a few years, with the most long-standing resident detectable for seven of the ten years of the study.

The martens of Galloway Forest, Scotland

For two reasons Galloway Forest in South-west Scotland has been the focus of pine marten research for many years: firstly, since the early 1990s, it was the most accessible marten population for marten-starved southerners like me; and secondly the forest is managed by Forest Enterprise Scotland (FES, an agency of the Forestry Commission), which has been extremely supportive of work to improve our collective understanding of pine marten ecology in a multi-purpose forest. The VWT first got involved in testing pine marten den boxes there in 2003 under the guidance of Geoff Shaw of FES, and with colleagues I have been visiting annually ever since.

There are now 100 den boxes of two different designs and we visit them annually to monitor pine marten breeding success.

We are learning much about the contribution that den boxes make to pine marten survival and breeding success in a modern forest, and especially about how breeding females use the boxes when we make our annual visits each May. We notice individual differences in the behaviour of adult females (some of which we have encountered in successive years): how they occupy the boxes; where they leave their scats and cache their prey; how they care for their kits; and how they interact with us when we inspect the boxes. These differences remind us that pine martens, like people, are not all the same; they have distinct patterns of behaviour and even 'personalities'.

Alongside our den box work, in autumn 2014 with Lizzie Croose we set out to count the number of pine martens in one part of Galloway Forest called the Fleet Basin, where we used non-invasive methods to gather scat and hair samples for genotyping. In an area of roughly 10,000 hectares we identified a minimum of 15 individuals (including sub-adults), with our modelling suggesting a maximum of 18 individuals; this represents a population density of 0.13–0.15 martens per square kilometre, so about 20 times lower than that found in Portlaw Woods. The estimated density of adult territory-holders only was lower still, at 0.08 per square kilometre, perhaps because the martens avoided areas affected by timber harvesting. With FES, we are keen to investigate how simple changes in forest management might help to boost marten numbers in the future.

HEALTH AND SAFETY

Causes of mortality
It is difficult to gather unbiased information on the relative contributions of different causes of pine marten mortality. Usually records are dominated by violent anthropogenic causes because these have been the easiest to detect, with little revealed about the impact of insidious anthropogenic deaths due to pollution and poisoning; nor do we know much about natural losses due to starvation, predation and disease. For example, Kathy Velander's record of the causes of death of 120 pine martens in Britain between 1960 and 1982 indicates that 64 per cent had been trapped, shot or snared, and a further 13 per cent were road casualties; the remaining 23 per cent were either 'unknown' or 'miscellaneous', which surely underplays the contribution of natural causes.

Despite their full legal protection, we know that pine martens are still injured or killed in spring traps deployed in ways that fail to exclude them; and doubtless they are deliberately or recklessly killed in other ways. This happens in those parts of Britain where predator control is ruthless and even protected predators are curiously absent or, at best, much scarcer than they should be. We cannot expect pine martens, with their very low reproductive rate, to establish and maintain healthy populations in such areas; so, this shameful issue needs to be resolved as soon as possible.

A proper assessment of natural fatalities can be identified only by expensive long-term radio-tracking studies in which carcasses can be recovered and autopsied to determine the cause of death. The VWT's monitoring of pine martens translocated to Wales, with full veterinary back-up, will provide much-needed information in due course; we have already learnt that at least two were killed by foxes.

Across Europe, pine martens may be killed by a wide range of predators other than foxes: wolf, lynx, wolverine, domestic dog, golden eagle, eagle owl, buzzard and goshawk are known or believed to predate adult martens; and marten kits may be taken by smaller woodland predators such as tawny and Ural owls. We explore below the prevalence of parasites and diseases that may afflict pine martens, sometimes with fatal consequences.

Street-fighting martens?

People who watch and feed pine martens in the Scottish Highlands have reported facial injuries on some of the martens they see, and I have seen nasty cuts on the muzzles of Scottish martens recorded on camera traps by the VWT. We don't currently know for certain what causes these injuries, but it is just possible that the increase in feeding of martens at dwellings has led to more frequent aggressive encounters as individuals compete for the tasty treats we provide for them; or perhaps martens have always beaten each other up but we are simply seeing the evidence more often because we are able to observe them more closely now. Irish photographer Maurice Flynn (who in 2015 won the Mammal Society's Mammal Photographer of the Year with a stunning shot of a leaping pine marten) witnessed a fierce attack by an adult male pine marten on a mother with two kits in Portlaw Woods in County Waterford: one kit was killed and the mother received two nasty cuts to her face.

Parasites and diseases

The growing interest in restoring populations of wild mammals, via reintroductions to areas from which they were removed many years ago, has encouraged a new focus on disease risk analysis to ensure that we minimise or avoid the accidental transfer of parasites, pathogens and diseases that might harm the new population and those of other species, including humans. This means that parasitologists and veterinarians are now valued collaborators in many mammal conservation projects. However, until very recently there have been very few studies of parasites and diseases in pine martens in Britain and Ireland, so we have to look beyond our shores for information.

In case there is in any doubt about the significance of martens as potential disease vectors, we need look no further than the 1980 study in California by Bill Zielinski in which pine martens (as the American marten is called there) tested positive for plague (*Yersinia pestis*), probably as a consequence of eating chipmunks and ground squirrels that are the usual wildlife reservoir of plague in that part of America. In central and eastern parts of Europe and in Russia both stone and pine martens are occasionally recorded as infected with the rabies virus: according to World Health Organisation published data for 2013 (in which the two marten species are not separated) rabies was found in small numbers of martens in Poland, the Russian Federation, Ukraine, Belarus and the Slovak Republic, for example. Beyond this low prevalence of rabies, other significant pathogens of the central nervous system have been recorded: in the Czech Republic infection by the widespread protozoan *Toxoplasma gondii* was found in the brain tissue of 17 per cent of pine martens sampled.

A rabies-related virus known as European bat lyssavirus (EBLV) is, as its name suggests, mainly found in bats in Europe, where the serotine *Eptesicus serotinus* is the main reservoir. However, it has been detected in a single stone marten in Germany, so transmission from infected bats to other mammals is possible but probably uncommon. As a general rule stone martens seem to pick up more interesting infections and diseases than do pine martens; this is very probably explained by their more urban lifestyle, which brings them into contact with a wider range of pathogens swilling about among our pets, domestic animals and discarded foodstuffs.

Starting with the ectoparasites found on pine martens, my friend Tim Hofmeester has kindly supplied new information from his PhD study of 53 road casualties collected from all over the Netherlands. He found that 85 per cent were parasitised by ticks, of which 1138 individuals of two species were identified: the sheep or deer tick (*Ixodes ricinus*) and the hedgehog tick (*Ixodes hexagonus*), which Paddy Sleeman suggested we should call the 'mustelid tick' in his 1989 Whittet book *Stoats and Weasels, Polecats and Martens* because it is found on so many members of the weasel family (Tim Hofmeester also found it on stone marten, badger and polecat, and others have recorded it on American mink and Eurasian otter). Tim's study is a useful reminder that, in addition to the large and highly visible adult female ticks protruding through the fur of their mammalian hosts, there is typically a numerically much greater burden of tick larvae and nymphs lurking less visibly beneath the fur.

The patterns of infestation of martens by the two tick species are rather different, and Hofmeester suggests this can best be explained by their contrasting behaviour and ecology: the infestation prevalence of *Ixodes ricinus* was 64 per cent (34 of 53 pine martens), with an average 15.6 ticks per individual; *Ixodes ricinus* was mainly found on pine martens in the summer half of the year because this is when the ticks lie in wait on vegetation for passing hosts, so pine martens encounter them as they move about on the woodland floor.

In contrast, *Ixodes hexagonus* gains access to its hosts by living in the dens and burrows where mammals sleep and breed, including the tree cavities occupied by pine martens in the Netherlands. The infestation prevalence of *Ixodes hexagonus* on pine martens was 51 per cent with an average intensity of infestation of 22.6 ticks per individual. Unlike *Ixodes ricinus* there was no seasonal infestation pattern – presumably because pine martens may encounter them in den sites at any time of year – and both sexes were heavily parasitised by this species. Hofmeester speculates that infestations of *Ixodes hexagonus* in pine marten natal dens may be one reason why mother martens typically move their kits to a new den at some point during the summer: adult female ticks lay their eggs after about two weeks of feasting on the blood of their host mammal, and the eggs hatch after two months; so two and a half months after the first blood meal by an adult female *Ixodes hexagonus* the den cavity would be infested by thousands of larval ticks, providing a strong incentive for a house-move by a responsible mother marten.

Sarcoptic mange or scabies is caused by a parasitic mite *Sarcoptes scabiei* that burrows into the skin of various mammals. Mainly found in wild foxes, it has been recorded in pine martens in Sweden, where many foxes were heavily infected during an outbreak in the late twentieth century. Three species of lice from the genus *Trichotedes* are known to infest martens of various species around the world; one of these, *Trichotedes retusa*, has been recorded on pine martens.

Pine martens also carry fleas. These were recorded by Tim Hofmeester on his Netherland martens, as well as by the VWT in its work on Scottish Highland pine martens – the species are awaiting identification in both cases as I write. In their review of fleas on Irish mammals, Paddy Sleeman and colleagues recorded only one species on the pine marten: *Monopsyllus sciurorum* (now known as *Ceratophyllis sciurorum*), which is normally found on its main host the red squirrel; so, this flea is likely to have arrived either via predation of the squirrel host by a marten, or by a marten resting in a flea-infested red squirrel drey. This squirrel flea is among three species detected on both pine and stone martens sampled much further east in the Czech Republic; it has also been found on pine martens in Croatia, Slovenia and Spain, so is likely to be quite widespread.

Beyond the itchily dubious delights of ectoparasitism, pine martens suffer a variety of other parasites and diseases, and I am grateful to my veterinary friend Kari-Anne Heald for gathering a toe-curling series of recent papers on the subject. Several smaller mustelids are prone to infection by the almost unpronounceable helminth nematodes of the genus *Skrjabingylus*. These 'sinus worms' have the beastly habit of taking up residence in the sinuses of their weasely hosts. There they show their gratitude by causing abscesses and damage to the skull, including perforations and, occasionally, abnormal bone growth. The most frequently encountered species in Britain and Ireland is *Skrjabingylus nasicola*, which is commonly found in stoats and weasels; but Peter Stuart and colleagues at the National University of Ireland, Galway, recently recorded an Irish pine marten infected with 23 specimens of *Skrjabingylus petrowi*. This species is commonly found in pine martens in the central and eastern parts of its Eurasian range, leading to suggestions that this species prefers the pine marten above all other mustelids as its host (although a recent survey of pine martens in Germany found a rather low prevalence of *Skrjabingylus petrowi*).

Pine martens support a variety of other helminth parasites – mostly nematodes but including occasional trematodes, cestodes and acanthocephalans – in their intestinal tracts and, because they generally arrive there as a result of their intermediate hosts being eaten by martens, this can give some unexpected insights into pine marten feeding ecology. For example, a study of helminths in the intestines of Spanish pine martens, by Juan-Matias Segovia and colleagues at the University of Barcelona, revealed 17 different species, with a high prevalence of three trichurid nematode species strongly suggesting that pine martens eat a lot of earthworms. This is an interesting revelation because it is easy to overlook the undigested remains of earthworms (their microscopic chaetae) in marten scats, so perhaps conventional dietary studies have underestimated or ignored the significance of earthworms?

A recent study by Maslennikova of helminths, in the carcasses of 87 pine martens harvested for their fur from the Kirov area of Russia, found 17 species, some of which had high prevalence rates: for example, the nematode *Aoncotheca putorii* was detected in 60 per cent of martens;

the sinus worm *Skrjabingylus petrowi* was found in 56 per cent; the aptly named nematode *Filaroides martis* was found in 54 per cent of pine martens (and widely in other studies of martens in North America and Europe); and the trematode *Alaria alata* was abundant in 48 per cent of those pine martens examined.

In south-western France, a serological survey by Christine Fournier-Chambrillon and colleagues of Aleutian disease (parvo)virus (ADV), mainly found in American mink and suspected for its possible role in the decline of European mink, revealed ADV antibodies in a single pine marten and two stone martens. Similarly, in Germany, antibodies to canine parvovirus (CPV) were found in both marten species by Kai Frölich and colleagues, although neither is suspected of playing a significant role in the transmission of CPV to domestic dogs.

Back in south-western France, the same team that conducted the ADV study above looked for evidence of Leptospirosis – a disease caused by pathogenic bacteria of the genus *Leptospira*. They found very high rates of exposure to *Leptospira* in all mustelids, including 89 per cent of stone martens and 74 per cent of pine martens; these unusually high exposure levels are believed to be related to the abundance of known reservoirs of *Leptospira* in that rather damp part of France, namely wetland rodents such as rats, coypu and muskrat. They also found antibodies to the potentially lethal Canine Distemper Virus (CDV) in 5 per cent of pine martens; however, CDV antibody prevalence was higher in both stone martens (33 per cent) and polecats (20 per cent), perhaps because their behaviour involves greater contact with domestic dogs.

Wildlife veterinarian Vic Simpson broke new ground when he and colleagues undertook post-mortems of four pine martens killed in road traffic accidents in the West Highlands of Scotland in the early 2000s. Adult and nymph stage ticks from three of the animals were identified as *Ixodes ricinus* and *ixodes hexagonus* (the same two species identified on Hofmeester's Dutch pine martens). Three of the pine martens revealed lesions in the heart and skeletal musculature consistent with the protozoan parasite *Hepatozoon*. One adult male had masses of large red *Skrjabingylus* nematodes in its maxillary sinuses and clusters of slender, hair-like nematodes (unidentified) attached to the mucosa of the trachea and bronchial tubes; and both this animal and an adult female had nematode clusters in their lungs. Vic Simpson is providing his specialist veterinary input to the VWT's reinforcement of the pine marten population in Wales, with a publication on pine marten health issues expected in the near future.

INTERACTIONS WITH OTHER WILDLIFE

Relations with foxes

Pine martens and red foxes co-occur over a wide area in which, as generalist carnivores both with a fondness for small rodents, they eat a very similar range of food, so there is great potential for competition. Andrzej Zalewski collaborated with József Lanszki and Gyözö Horváth in a study of the feeding ecology of both species in a Hungarian deciduous forest. They found that rodents dominated the diets of both predators, and both showed a preference for bank voles and consumed fewer Apodemus mice and shrews than expected (based upon their availability).

Red foxes sometimes kill pine martens as competitors, so escape routes are very important where there is a risk of a foxy encounter.

At times of low rodent abundance foxes and pine martens were adept at switching to alternative types of food, such as ungulate carcasses, birds, fruit and invertebrates. Although there were subtle differences in the food consumed, there was substantial dietary overlap between them. So how does this influence their relationship?

Writing in 1892, Macpherson summed up the tense relationship between foxes and pine martens in Britain as 'Foxes and Martens do not flourish very well on the same ground'; and he quotes the Lakeland hunters' saying, 'When Foxes is rank, Marts is scarce'. Studies in Scandinavia by Erik Lindström and Jan Olof Helldin reveal that foxes commonly kill pine martens as competitors and this mortality may limit marten populations. Closer to home, during the course of the VWT's Pine Marten Recovery Project, two of the adult Scottish martens translocated to Wales were apparently killed by foxes after their release.

So, on our islands, where foxes are relatively abundant and our woodland cover is low and highly fragmented, pine martens may have an especially tough time. We need research on this topic to help us understand how it might influence the recovery of marten populations. At the very least we should expect pine martens to behave in ways that reduce the risk of dangerous encounter with foxes. For example, pine martens are likely to avoid those areas where foxes are most abundant, such as lowland farmland and suburbia. They should prefer those habitats offering abundant escape opportunities and dens out of the reach of foxes, such as mature woodland with elevated tree-holes. They might adjust their activity patterns so as to avoid periods when foxes are most active; and marten dispersal between scattered woodlands may be constrained by the constant risk of foxy attacks. Equally, we might expect pine martens to survive rather well where foxes are heavily controlled, so long as the control methods don't clobber martens as well.

Sometimes, however, the tables turn, and there is one reliable report of a pine marten killing fox cubs while their mother was absent. In April to June 2013 Marcin Brzeziński and colleagues were using three camera traps to film badger activity at a woodland sett just outside the Lake Łuknajno Biosphere Reserve in north-east Poland. A detailed record of mammal activity was made, which first revealed the badgers moving out to leave a vixen and her cubs as the sole occupants; after a few nights a pine marten was recorded making an early morning visit to the sett, followed by a late evening visit when it entered the sett and emerged with a live fox cub in its mouth, which it then killed in full view of one of the cameras and carried off. The pine marten returned four minutes later and quickly entered the sett, emerging a minute later with another fox cub that it carried off into the forest.

Adjusting to the return of a native predator

We are fast learning that historical removal of a predator from an ecosystem can have all sorts of consequences beyond the obvious one of boosting the survival and breeding success of certain prey species such as game birds. We don't usually appreciate these until the predator is finally allowed to recover, but we can make some assumptions. For example, the absence of the pine marten from most British woodlands in the late 1800s – and rather later in Ireland – must have made it easier for the alien grey squirrel to establish itself much more quickly and completely than it would otherwise have done (more on pine marten impacts on grey squirrels below); and another exotic arboreal rodent, the edible dormouse, probably could not exist at the high densities it does currently in woodlands on and around the Chilterns if pine martens had been present. If it was good enough for the Romans to eat I am sure our pine martens would have willingly tucked into this chunky, squirrel-sized dormouse. So, our earlier removal of a native arboreal predator has almost certainly helped two exotic pests to become established to wreak havoc in our woodlands.

The pine marten does not always hold the upper paw in predator-prey interactions, however: Scottish camera trap footage from April 2017 by photographer Chas Moonie shows an adult pine marten up a tree being attacked and knocked to the ground by the talons of a swooping tawny owl. This extraordinary footage suggests that tawny owls recognise pine martens both as a threat to their own kind and as competitors in the quest for small rodent prey on the woodland floor.

How do pine martens and stone martens coexist?

It is unusual for two species like the pine and stone marten – that are very similar in size, shape and ecology – to be able to coexist in the long-term over such a large shared range. The table below shows that within each gender Polish stone and pine martens are very similar in body length, but stone martens are slightly heavier so their body mass index is greater at 16.94 than that of pine martens at 13.58. Nevertheless, these differences are so slight that they are most unlikely to limit competition for resources, so there must be some other processes operating.

The only way in which coexistence between stone and pine martens can be maintained is by one or both species adjusting their behaviour in order to reduce competition. We would predict that this must involve some detectable differences between the two species in one or more of the following elements of behaviour: habitat use, diet, or the timing of activity. Studies from various parts of Europe confirm that pine and stone martens do indeed behave differently in most of these respects.

Species	Sex	Body weight		Body length (i.e. excluding tail)
		Mean	Range	Mean
Stone marten	Female	1.23	1.08–1.42	42.04
	Male	1.5	1.22–1.78	44.45
Pine marten	Female	0.96	0.79–1.12	41.7
	Male	1.32	0.95–1.65	46.1

Body weights and lengths of 46 stone martens and 27 pine martens from Białowieża Forest. (Data from Anna Wereszczuk and Andrzej Zalewski of the Polish Academy of Sciences)

Many studies have shown that stone and pine martens use the landscape in rather different ways. Stone martens clearly prefer human-modified landscapes, including farmland, farmsteads, villages, towns and cities; in this respect, they are the most urban of all European mustelids, with recent studies confirming the widespread presence of populations in large cities such as Krakow and Budapest. In contrast, pine martens show a clear preference for woodland and tend to avoid open areas well away from woodland. The most useful information on habitat segregation has come from research based on radio-tracking both marten species in the same study area at the same time. One such project was recently undertaken in Białowieża Forest by Anna Wereszczuk and Andrzej Zalewski of the Polish Academy of Sciences. Analysis of more than 6,000 radio locations from 21 stone martens and 13 pine martens revealed that each species occupied completely different habitats within the forest ecosystem: stone martens mainly occupied the villages within the forest, as well as a few open habitats surrounding them such as meadows and non-wooded wetlands; pine martens were found only in wooded habitats (deciduous, coniferous and wet woodlands) and nowhere else.

This segregation in use of habitats is a most effective way of avoiding competition because it means that each species tends to forage for food in different places and, because some prey populations also show habitat preferences, it may lead to dietary segregation too. It is suggested that this habitat segregation arose because the stone marten conceded the favoured woodland option to the pine marten and used its greater adaptability to exploit the new open landscapes created by early humans as it moved north into Europe from its origins in the Middle East. This idea is supported by evidence from those parts of southern Europe where pine martens are absent – such as southern Iberia – in which stone martens commonly occupy wooded habitats such as cork oak woodland, presumably because of freedom from competition with the other marten.

Anthony Clevenger reviewed published studies of the diets of stone martens (14 studies) and pine martens (15 studies) across Europe. As we would expect from two such opportunistic predators, their diets appeared to reflect local food availability. There was considerable dietary overlap between the two species, which had similar food niche breadths and took prey of similar sizes (although in some studies there was a tendency for pine martens to take larger prey than did stone martens). But within their broadly similar diets there were some crucial differences in emphasis: for example, mammals were the most important prey group in 11 out of 15 pine marten diets and in four out of 14 stone marten diets; in contrast vegetation (mainly fruit) was the dominant food category in seven stone marten diets and in only two of the pine marten diets. In fact, the stone marten is the most frugivorous of all the carnivores in Europe.

Investigating another element of habitat use, a study in the Bresse Region of eastern France revealed that stone and pine martens used quite different resting sites: whereas nearly all (98 per cent) of the pine martens' dens were in woodlands, 83 per cent of the stone martens' dens were in open habitats close to human habitations; so, by this means they avoided competing for resting and breeding sites.

Finally, Dutch and Polish research has shown that stone martens are more strictly nocturnal than pine martens and their activity peaked at different times, which might help further to reduce competition by introducing a time-partitioning element to foraging by each species. However, surely the major benefit of being strictly nocturnal is that it enables stone martens to live and breed in towns and cities undetected by their human residents. Furthermore, it is likely that human persecution has influenced pine marten activity patterns, forcing that species to be more nocturnal than it might otherwise need to be and, thereby, limiting the time-partitioning element of competition avoidance.

So, thanks largely to their preference for different habitats within modern landscapes, stone and pine martens are able to coexist over their extensive common range in Europe. This situation should continue so long as those landscapes provide a mix of woodland blocks, farmland and urban spaces. And in those areas where one species is missing – stone martens in the north and pine martens in parts of the south – we might expect the other species to enjoy a less constrained pattern of habitat use. This includes Britain and Ireland of course, where the (recent only?) absence of the stone marten must have made it easier for pine martens to survive those lean times in the late 1800s when woodland cover fell below 5 per cent; and now breeding female pine martens are free to rear their kits in our roof voids just as stone martens do on the continent.

However, we cannot take this current situation for granted, for the reality of global climate change has led to a worryingly one-sided prediction about the future coexistence of these two martens. This arises because they have different climatic adaptations: whereas pine martens are cold-adapted, stone martens are thermophilic (meaning they like it warm). As well as explaining the more northerly distribution of the pine marten, this difference warns us that the pine marten could be the loser in our warming world, as suggested by two recent studies below.

Maria Vergara and colleagues undertook a modelling study to improve our understanding of pine and stone marten coexistence in Iberia, at the south-western edge of their area of overlap in Europe. They developed habitat suitability models that confirmed not just different habitat selection by each species, but also different responses to climatic variables, so that in places where both species occurred, pine martens were associated with cooler areas and stone martens preferred the warmer ones. Running their models through different climate change scenarios, Vergara's team found that pine martens were predicted to decline markedly by the mid-twenty-first century as the extent of those cooler areas contracted, while stone martens were expected to benefit as the extent of their favoured warm areas expanded.

So, as our global climate continues to heat up, we have to expect the southern limits of the pine marten's global range to shrink northwards in common with other cold-adapted species. This was the conclusion reached in a wider modelling exercise by Joshua Lawler and colleagues, which predicted substantial range contraction for the pine marten especially in the south-western and eastern parts of its European range. The model also predicted some contraction in the stone marten's range – especially in southern Iberia – but, unlike the pine marten, the stone marten was predicted also to enjoy some large areas of range expansion to the north of its current range as presently cool areas warm up. Thus, on balance, the stone marten should be a winner and the pine marten a loser in the likely scenario of we humans failing miserably to prevent further global warming.

Capercaillie capers

The capercaillie is a huge, impressive bird that has recently been drawn into the debate about whether pine martens in Scotland should be controlled. The largest member of the grouse family, the capercaillie thrives in conifer forests across northern Europe, where pine martens have been eating its eggs and chicks for thousands of years with no adverse impact upon its status and distribution. In Scotland, the capercaillie is now faring less well, and its latest decline (it is known to have gone extinct once already and was reintroduced in 1837 using Swedish birds) has given hope to those desperate to see the pine marten labelled as a 'problem predator'. Since its late-twentieth century recovery in Scotland there have been calls for the pine marten's legal protection to be removed so that stocks of pheasants, red grouse and red-legged partridges can be better protected for game shooting. How convenient it would be if such a move could gain added conservation legitimacy by implicating the pine marten in the caper's decline.

Since the capercaillie's latest Scottish decline started in the mid-1970s (significantly this preceded the pine marten's re-establishment in the capercaillie's stronghold in north-east Scotland), there has been a great deal of research designed to tease out the causes and identify solutions. Capercaillie survival and breeding success are influenced by many factors, among which habitat and weather seem to be the most important: woodlands that are small, fragmented and damaged by deer browsing are bad for capercaillie, as are changes in temperature patterns in April that affect plant growth and reduce the condition of capercaillie hens, and wet weather in June that reduces chick survival; other pressures include disturbance by walkers and skiers, and collisions when adults fly into deer fences (installed, ironically, to improve forest habitat by reducing deer browsing); and finally, predation of eggs and chicks by foxes, corvids, raptors and pine martens can reduce breeding success.

Despite exhaustive statistical analyses, the pine marten's role in the capercaillie's plight emerges as peripheral at most. The most rigorous evidence indicates that changing weather patterns in Scotland leading to the miss-timing of hen food availability in April and wetter Junes that kill chicks – very likely driven by climate change – are key to the capercaillie's poor breeding success in recent decades.

Perhaps because we cannot do much about the weather, and despite the pine marten's legal protection and its peripheral role in the capercaillie's decline, since 2012 the Game and Wildlife Conservation Trust (GWCT) has proposed a trial removal of pine martens in the capercaillie's stronghold in north-east Scotland. This is intended to be a scientific study designed to gather evidence of the benefits to capercaillie of removing all pine martens from selected forests in which these two protected species occur. However, the legal removal of pine martens would require a licence from Scottish Natural Heritage and no such licence has yet been granted. Nevertheless, publicity about the removal trial has inevitably spread across Scotland, promoting the flawed idea that removing pine martens might be a justifiable response to a complex ecological issue – something that will do pine martens no good where people are willing to ignore the law intended to protect them.

PINE MARTENS | INTERACTIONS WITH OTHER WILDLIFE

Thankfully there are others involved in capercaillie conservation who have been willing to seek solutions beyond the traditional obsession with removing predators. Within the capercaillie's core Scottish range in Strathspey, FES has been quietly working to improve its management of woodlands so as to achieve several objectives, including timber production, human recreation and wildlife conservation. In 2016, FES reported that the number of displaying male capercaillie had 'surged' seven-fold over 15 years in response to careful thinning of the forests in Strathspey, with improved habitat boosting chick survival, despite the presence of pine martens and other predators. Importantly, FES does not interfere with the predator community in its forests, and it reports that capercaillie have increased and bred well despite increases in both the number of predators and the number of predator species. FES staff speculate that there is an element of self-regulation in the predator community in their forests, with the activity of martens and corvids constrained by healthy populations of foxes and goshawks respectively (although the predator community may still be out of kilter as we shall discuss below). As well as being good news for capercaillie conservation, this forest management approach neatly challenges the dogma that clobbering predators is the only way to go to save a bird that, sadly, is probably doomed for quite different reasons to do with our changing climate.

Where a reduction in natural predation is desirable, this can still be achieved without removing predators. For example, in Finland hunters have for years used simple visual and chemical deterrent measures at nests of ground-nesting birds such as capercaillie and black grouse to protect them from predation by foxes and pine martens. Apparently, this can be very successful, so the same enlightened FES team that boosted capercaillie numbers in Strathspey by tweaking forest management is now planning to investigate the traditional Finnish nest protection measures to increase capercaillie chick production yet further. Good luck to them!

One final piece of the capercaillie predation jigsaw is 'meso-predator release', which means the increased abundance and/or activity of medium-sized predators that occurs after larger apex predators (such as Eurasian lynx and wolf) have been removed by humans. It is possible that this has resulted in increased predation at capercaillie nests in parts of Europe, although pine marten numbers may actually be suppressed where foxes become more abundant in the absence of apex predators. Nevertheless, this suggests that a natural and sustainable solution to reducing predation at capercaillie nests by foxes and martens, where evidence indicates it is excessive, is to restore missing components of the predator guild.

That was one conclusion reached after a recent Spanish study of capercaillie in the Pyrenees conducted by Rubén Moreno-Opo and colleagues. They demonstrated that capercaillie breeding success could be improved by humans removing pine martens, stone martens and red foxes on an annual basis. However, they also recognised that this interventionist approach was very costly, ecologically unsustainable and ethically questionable. Far better, the authors suggested, to restore an apex predator such as the Eurasian lynx to achieve the same reduction in mesocarnivore numbers naturally, for ever and for free. We can be optimistic that it would work because this effect has been observed in Finland, where natural recovery of the Eurasian lynx population led to a decline in foxes and increased abundance of forest grouse, including capercaillie. Currently there are plans to reintroduce the lynx to parts of Scotland and northern England, though whether this can save the capercaillie from further decline due to the overriding influence of climate change is doubtful.

Grey squirrel control?
Thanks to the Victorians' passion for importing alien mammals to rural estates because this might make them look a bit more interesting, our woodlands and their wildlife have been suffering at the hands (or teeth, to be strictly accurate) of the North American grey squirrel ever since. Grey squirrels have caused serious damage to commercial broadleaf timber-growing interests (with losses estimated at £10 million a year in Britain); and the forestry industry has struggled and failed to come up with a cost-effective means of controlling the species.

Also, since the early 1900s, grey squirrels have been outcompeting our native red squirrels and steadily replacing them in our woodlands, first in southern Britain and rather later in Ireland. As if that wasn't bad enough, more recently the greys in northern England and southern Scotland have been carrying a 'squirrel pox' virus that is relatively harmless to greys but is fatal to red squirrels. Both timber growers and wildlife conservationists had effectively admitted defeat in their battle with the greys, with some reluctantly predicting that, in the long-term, wild red squirrels would be safe only on offshore islands. Then someone noticed something happening out west to raise their flagging spirits.

In Ireland, something rather exciting – marten-wise – emerged as the last century drew to a close: a handful of foresters and landowners noticed that, as pine martens recolonised woodlands in the Irish Midlands (from which they had been exterminated by humans a few decades earlier), the non-native grey squirrels mysteriously disappeared and the red squirrels that had earlier been pushed out by the greys then made a welcome return, despite the continued presence of pine martens.

I first heard about this curious effect from my Welsh forester friend

Huw Denman, who told me how a client of his was thrilled when the pesky grey squirrels mysteriously vanished from his woodland in County Laois in about 1995, just after pine martens reappeared, and then his beloved red squirrels came back soon afterwards. I was excited on at least two fronts: firstly, it was good to hear that a native predator recovering its numbers should apparently lead to the decline of a non-native pest, with a beleaguered native – the red squirrel – seemingly benefiting as a consequence; equally exciting was the prospect of a re-working of long-established negative attitudes among landowners towards predators and predation. Although this effect was reported from other Irish woodlands, before it would be taken seriously we needed evidence that was more than anecdotal, and above all we needed some understanding of what exactly was going on between greys, reds and martens in the Irish Midlands; and that meant we needed some proper research.

Colin Lawton at the National University of Ireland, Galway secured funding for a PhD study and in 2011 his student Emma Sheehy started to study the interactions between pine martens and red and grey squirrels in the Irish Midlands. The work involved distribution surveys of each species that confirmed the anecdotal reports of pine martens having expanded their range, while the grey squirrel population had crashed over the same area and red squirrels were common again after an absence of up to 30 years. Importantly Sheehy demonstrated that, at a landscape scale, the abundance of pine martens and red squirrels was positively correlated, while the presence of pine martens and grey squirrels in woodlands was strongly negatively correlated. This led Sheehy and Lawton to speculate that the pine marten could be a critical factor in determining the success or failure of grey squirrel populations. There is still much to learn about the nature and mechanism of this effect, but interestingly a study in Northern Ireland by Dave Tosh suggests that grey squirrels are much more naïve than reds when it comes to the scent of pine martens.

Dubbed 'the Sheehy Effect', the Irish pine marten's beneficial role in driving out grey squirrels – thus enabling red squirrels to thrive again – gave new hope to timber growers and red squirrel conservationists on the British mainland. Might recovering pine marten populations perform a free biological control operation on grey squirrels and so allow foresters to grow thin-barked broadleaved timber again? And could they drive grey squirrel populations down below the threshold required for them to spread the pox virus to the beleaguered reds? Although the processes driving these welcome changes are not yet fully understood, it does seem as if the re-establishment of a healthy pine marten population creates what ecologists call a 'Landscape of Fear' in which grey squirrels fail to thrive.

Anecdotal evidence from 2010 onwards suggested that the Sheehy Effect might be operating in parts of Scotland where pine martens had expanded their range into the grey squirrel zone. And further work by Emma Sheehy in southern Scotland during 2015–2016 suggested that the effect did seem to be operating there. This has led scientists at Heriot-Watt and Edinburgh Universities to model the extent to which pine marten predation might reduce the costs of grey squirrel control designed to protect red squirrels in southern Scotland; the initial results are encouraging.

Traditional trap-based methods of grey squirrel control – used in many woodlands by those protecting either timber or red squirrels – are a cause for concern in Wales now because of the risk they pose to the newly invigorated pine marten population following the VWT's translocation of Scottish martens. Pine martens are very likely to enter any peanut-baited trap set for squirrels, and the prime period for catching grey squirrels – March to June – coincides exactly with when hungry lactating female martens would be most vulnerable to capture, leading to the possible starvation of their dependent kits. Therefore, the VWT's staff in Wales are urging squirrel trappers either to use traps that exclude martens, or to check their traps more frequently – at least twice per day – and preferably to close them down at night so as to minimise impacts upon the precious pine marten population.

Also in Wales, during 2015 to 2017 PhD student Catherine McNichol studied the effects of the VWT's translocated pine martens upon the local grey squirrel population. Already it is clear that grey squirrels are being killed and eaten by the martens, and in due course McNichol's analysis should reveal more about the nature and scale of interactions between these two species.

INTERACTIONS WITH PEOPLE

The teething pains of pine marten recovery
Human attitudes towards the recovery of pine martens in Britain and Ireland are very polarised and directly influenced by people's commercial and recreational interests, as well as by more visceral reactions. On the negative side (there are positives further below), in parts of the Irish Midlands where pine martens have recently made a healthy recovery, the National Parks and Wildlife Service (NPWS) rangers report public perceptions of a 'plague' of martens; in 2016 farmers in Counties Longford and Donegal called for a cull of pine martens to protect sheep flocks; in Britain, the Scottish Gamekeepers' Association has called – unsuccessfully so far – for the pine marten's legal protection to be removed so that its members are free to protect their pheasants and grouse in traditional ways; and subsequently the GWCT has argued in favour of a 'trial removal' of pine martens to protect the declining capercaillie (see *Capercaillie capers*, page 150). Whether or not these arguments deserve to be taken seriously, it is important to understand the real motivations behind them, though this is not the place for such serious psychoanalysis.

In a bizarre twist to this sorry tale, the recovering pine marten's protected status – and that of other predators – is proving to be the perfect gift for lazy or incompetent land managers: some cannot resist the temptation to shift the blame for their husbandry failures on to one or other 'untouchable' protected species; and if this also helps to turn public opinion against the old enemy, so much the better!

Mischievous media manipulation
Modern antipathy towards pine martens – typically rooted in the Victorian anti-predator legacy and a land manager's fear of 'not being in control' in the face of a recovering protected species – fuels desperate attempts to manipulate public opinion by spreading 'scare stories' in the press and media. Though it has been happening in the Scottish Highlands for years, the worst examples recently have come from the Irish Midlands, where one or two members of the farming community seem intent on branding pine martens as a serious threat to livestock and even people. Irish farming press headlines in 2016 such as 'Pine marten attacks sheep

in Longford' and 'He killed her chicken and bit her, she had to get a tetanus shot – Residents say once-rare pine martens are out of control' are followed by evidence-thin rants about losses of livestock and predictions that children could be at risk. Journalists must take much of the blame for publishing stories based on extreme opinions without first checking the evidence, seeking alternative views and offering sensible, sustainable solutions to any genuine conflicts.

Such awful, one-sided journalism is reminiscent of the 1960s and 1970s when American mink were spreading in Britain and generating scare stories as only an 'invading alien predator' could. While I was studying wild mink for my PhD in the late 1970s I collected examples of newspaper cuttings, among which 'Mink attack horses' was my favourite. So, when reading about pine martens in the popular press please be alert to possible manipulation of the media. And farming journalists, please pull your socks up!

The good, the bad and the delightfully cheeky
Being slim, inquisitive, nocturnal climbers with omnivorous tastes, pine martens are perfectly designed to be a nuisance to we humans from time to time; but their mischief is delivered with an impish charm that disarms all but the most hard-hearted person; and their sylvan grace and beauty embody a fragile wild spirit that many of us long to connect with as an antidote to the stresses of modern life. With their cute appeal, pine martens have the wildlife X-Factor: they are still rare or absent in many parts of our islands, so naturalists and photographers migrate keenly to marten-rich areas in the hope of a sighting or, at the very least, a sniff of fresh marten scats!

For those who live in those parts of Ireland and Scotland where pine martens are, at last, common once more, there are myriad human stories of people's interactions with them and the attitudes they hold as a consequence. These range from the soft-hearted Irish restaurateur who bought a ruined cottage on the Burren to save it from development just so that his local pine martens could continue to breed in its roof; through the Royal Deeside gamekeeper who predicted the extinction of red squirrels because of the menace of pine martens, and argued that their legal protection should be removed so that he could protect his game in the traditional ways; to the sleep-deprived householder who struggled to tolerate the thumps and bumps above his bedroom ceiling while a mother marten taught her kits to catch the live prey she had released into the roof void; and finally to the elderly Scottish couple on the Black Isle near Inverness whose lives are hugely enriched by the martens that visit their house in the woods to enjoy the nightly feast of food set out for them.

Pine martens adore sweet foods and there are many stories of them breaking into properties and causing mayhem in pursuit of their sugary passion. One Christmas in Argyll, a marten repeatedly broke into a village shop after closing time and feasted on mince pies, opening a fresh box each night until the owner live-trapped it and relocated it tens of kilometres away (from where someone later sent a postcard to the shop owner that read 'Having a lovely time, wish you were here – P. Marten'). Also in Argyll, a pine marten came down the chimney to feast on leftovers in a hotel kitchen; when the chef arrived next morning, he found his precious kitchen in a state of chaos, with even more breakages occurring as he tried to evict the over-fed marten with a broom. And one night a pine marten raided a cake cabinet inside a ski-slope restaurant high up in the Nevis Range in Scotland where, having eaten all it could manage, it hid the rest of the cakes in odd places all over the building. The staff told me that for days afterwards they kept finding bits of cake under cushions, chairs and cupboards, and they knew the marten was still visiting because they saw its muddy footprints on the tables and leather sofas. Much, much later, shocked diners witnessed a rock-hard, mouldy bread roll mysteriously falling to the floor from its hiding place high up in the rafters – fortunately no one was hurt.

A favourite story told to me by Matt Wilson involves a pine marten that came close to causing a fist-fight among a group of grown men who had chartered a boat for a diving holiday at Lochaline in the West of Scotland. After an evening's drinking the divers were in the habit of sharing biscuits over a cup of tea around the kitchen table before withdrawing to their bunks for the night. On rising the next morning, they discovered all the biscuits had gone and the table was left in an awful mess; and the cupboards were left hanging open and further food was missing. As the boat left the harbour for the next day's dive, the morning air was filled with vehement accusations and vigorous denials among the divers; but the same thing happened the next night and the one after, causing further conflict and threatening to ruin the entire holiday. Finally, after suspicions arose that a furry party might be involved, the boat owner asked Matt to identify the culprit. He used a camera trap to confirm that a pine marten was in the habit of stepping off the pier to visit the boat late at night to steal food as the 'over-tired' divers slept; the marten had even excavated a den in the bulkhead down in the engine hold so that sometimes it slept soundly on board while accompanying the divers on their day trips out to sea.

Sugar-related invasions are not the end of it; pine martens make a nuisance of themselves in many other ways, such as predation of poultry and game, thefts of eggs and garden fruit, noisy breeding in roof voids and messy raiding of dustbins. Often their mischief is harmless and simply raises a smile, like the report on BBC Radio 4's Today programme in early August 2016: a family of four pine martens – most likely a mother and three kits – had taken up residence inside Scottish Power's underground hydroelectric power station at Cruachan beside Loch Awe near Oban in north-west Scotland. Nicknamed the 'Loch Awe Four', the pine martens entertained power station staff and visitors by accepting snacks and even hopping on to the tour bus several times to join visitors on trips around the site.

Adapting to life with pine martens

People are already developing sensible ways of responding to the new challenges presented by mischievous pine martens, so that they can live alongside them in something approaching harmony. For example, you may have wondered why, across the Scottish Highlands, many rural householders place heavy rocks on top of their council 'wheelie-bins': it is not just to prevent powerful Highland winds from lifting the lids and scattering domestic waste across the neighbourhood; it is also to prevent the local pine martens from doing the same, for in many areas they have learnt the clever trick of climbing on to the top of a bin and getting inside to sample the contents by lifting the very lid they are standing on. Thanks to the VWT, in Ireland there is an alternative measure being used, involving a tough strap that wraps around the entire bin from top to bottom – very handy if you happen to live in an area short of rocks.

This bin protection measure is just one example of how people are adapting to life with pine martens where the species has finally been allowed to become common again; it is also, to me, a hopeful symbol of tolerance and a sign of a willingness to resolve conflicts in intelligent, sustainable ways, rather than asking the local gamekeeper to get rid of the martens in the old way – which still happens of course, but doesn't solve the problem long-term.

Because pine martens like eating fruit, there are many stories from Scotland of them harvesting raspberries, gooseberries, strawberries and plums just before the owners intended to gather these for themselves. Electric fencing around fruit cages and poly tunnels has been used successfully to deter pine martens so that gardeners can get to their fruit first. In both Ireland and Scotland, the VWT has collaborated with relevant organisations to produce a free leaflet *Living with Pine Martens* that summarises the various measures that enable people to resolve conflicts with pine martens in legal and sustainable ways (see Further reading, page 189).

Protecting bird boxes
People like putting up bird boxes and sometimes these actually help bird populations by providing a valuable resource – sheltered, elevated cavities suitable for nesting in – that is otherwise scarce or absent. The trouble with bird boxes is that they also make it much easier for predators to locate and predate bird nests by providing them with a simple search image to focus upon – like a series of well-stocked lunch boxes stuck up

trees – so clutches of eggs are much easier to find than those in natural nest sites. Sometimes mammalian predators such as pine martens are helped to find bird boxes by following the scent of us larger 'predators', although human 'predation' these days tends to involve only weighing and ringing chicks. So, unless they are very cleverly camouflaged and not visited closely by humans, bird boxes may lead to an increase in predation rates upon breeding birds – and similar effects may apply to boxes installed for other species such as bats and dormice.

Not surprisingly, ornithologists report that pine martens frequently find and raid bird boxes, causing losses of eggs and chicks and sometimes killing the incubating adults too. Although the impact of this predation upon bird populations is unknown and may well be insignificant, it is distressing to those operating bird box schemes, especially when rare or vulnerable species are affected. In the case of nest boxes designed for larger birds such as goldeneye and owls, pine martens can enter to remove the eggs one by one; and with smaller boxes designed for birds such as pied flycatchers, the martens may destroy a clutch of eggs or kill the chicks by poking a forelimb through the small entrance hole to rake through the nest in an attempt to extract a meal.

Thanks to some lateral thinking by a few clever people, there are solutions that substantially reduce the impact of pine marten predation at bird boxes, and sometimes this simply involves using materials that pine martens cannot climb. On Speyside in north-east Scotland, Allan Bantick recorded pine martens climbing up trees to steal eggs from his goldeneye boxes, so he relocated the nest boxes on to the tops of long shiny plastic sewage pipes buried end-on into the ground. Next spring the goldeneyes didn't mind nesting in boxes on shiny 'trees' with no branches; and the pine martens failed to climb up to the boxes so the eggs were safe from one predator at least. In central Scotland, Dave Anderson of FES applied the same principle by fitting sheets of shiny anti-climb plastic or metal around tree trunks to prevent martens climbing up to bird boxes or to the natural nests of vulnerable birds. To reduce the pine martens' access to smaller bird boxes, people have experimented successfully with alternative ways of fitting them to trees: some have hung them from branches on lengths of wire that keep them out of the pine martens' reach. So, yet again, there are ingenious but low-tech solutions to a common problem.

Roof martens

An increasing challenge presented by pine martens in both Ireland and Scotland is their tendency to breed inside the roofs of buildings, including people's houses and other properties such as hotels. Since the late twentieth century female pine martens have reacted to the scarcity of elevated dens in woodland tree cavities by breeding in roof voids, where they find the same tree-cavity conditions of protection from predators, shelter from weather and insulation against extreme temperatures that they need to raise their kits. Just like many bat colonies that are now dependent upon our roofs for roost sites, martens have been forced to 'follow the timber' in response to our harvesting of woodland trees. Roof voids bring the extra advantage of a much larger, safer space than is usually available in a cavity high up in a tree, with a variety of cosy places for sleeping among loft insulation, play areas for kits and toilet areas all literally under the same roof. This makes roof voids especially attractive to breeding female martens and, unless they are moved on by their human cohabitants, marten families tend to occupy them for longer periods than more natural breeding dens. While a mother marten typically moves her kits from a natal den in a tree cavity or den box to a new den site in late May, a family may occupy the same roof void through June and into July.

This roof-breeding behaviour, which is typical of the stone marten in continental Europe, was uncommon before legal protection led to reduced persecution of pine martens during the 1980s and subsequent expansion of populations into areas with higher human populations. Initially, because of the wariness associated with persecution, it probably involved pine martens mainly breeding in barns, outhouses and abandoned cottages, rather than in occupied dwelling houses. Nowadays, and especially since the 1990s, it has become increasingly common for pine martens to breed in the roofs of occupied houses, with some challenging behaviour to test the tolerance of human residents. Non-breeding adults may also occupy dens in houses, but they tend to make less noise and mess so don't attract so much attention. As with the pine martens' surprisingly extensive use of non-wooded habitats considered above, it is doubtful whether their now frequent use of buildings as resting and breeding sites would have been possible if the stone marten – mustelid master of urban living and cohabitation with humans – had (still?) been present on these islands.

An adult female marten may select her breeding den as early as February, when nights are long and cold, so humans tend to vegetate indoors, meaning she can usually enter and leave a roof void den undetected. Sometimes a marten has to enlarge an existing hole in a rotten soffit to improve access at the eaves, but otherwise there is usually little evidence of a new resident in the roof void – at least to start with. In late winter, hotels and holiday cottages are especially quiet, and this simple fact may explain why pine martens appear to prefer them as breeding sites over other types of dwelling; the mother marten is pretty quiet and unobtrusive too as she prepares to give birth in March or April; and then everything goes wrong when fee-paying guests arrive for a holiday in May or June just as the marten family is at its most rumbustious.

From mid-May onwards, the kits become more playful and start to explore their 'nursery' above the bedroom ceilings, with audible bumps and thumps at all times of day and night. As well as an increase in noise there can be smells arising from droppings and urine – which may soak through to stain ceilings below – as well as the whiff of unconsumed prey remains brought into the roof by the mother when she weans her kits in May. This combination of unwelcome noises and smells is usually enough to stretch the tolerance of humans in the living space below to breaking point, especially if they have paid good money for a precious, peaceful week's holiday in rural Ireland or the Scottish Highlands, but worse is yet to come!

As the kits become more agile and their physical confidence grows, usually in June, their doting mother starts to bring live prey into the roof for them to practice catching late at night. I remember talking to a sleep-deprived – but still remarkably tolerant – resident of the Highlands who was at his wits end after many nights listening to three marten kits chasing live rabbits and pigeons around in his roof at two o'clock in the morning. He had no intention of excluding the family, so his commendably big-hearted response was to sleep in a tent in the garden until the marten family moved out in July.

Although the ideal solution is to wait until the marten family leaves of its own accord before blocking up all access holes, not everyone is willing or able to tolerate the disturbance for that length of time, so anxious householders tend to appeal for urgent help with evicting the martens as soon as possible. Because pine martens are protected by law, marten families cannot be disturbed or evicted from dwelling houses without a licence – and even then, it is best to involve expert help and advice – so the relevant government authorities are usually the first port of call.

The staff of SNH in Scotland and NPWS in Ireland report that the number of calls to remove marten families from roof voids is increasing each year. Both organisations are developing humane ways to encourage a mother marten to move her young to a new denning site where householders are unwilling to wait for them to leave. Experience shows that the worst thing is to stress the mother so much that she deserts her young. This tends to happen if she is live-trapped during the eviction process, leaving her kits to be reared by human carers. So, it is very important that any householders contact their local office of NPWS or SNH for advice; and the VWT has collaborated with both organisations in the production of a useful free leaflet (see *Further reading*, page 189).

In many cases householders are happy to tolerate their marten family until it moves on in mid- to late summer, often taking great interest in the development of the kits and sometimes making adaptations to their properties to make life easier for the martens. For example, in 2016 a (human) family in Moray, north-east Scotland fitted a plastic cover above the martens' roof den entrance hole so that the mother could look out without getting wet when it rained (they called it her conservatory); and this also kept the timbers dry around the entrance hole so that the kits were less likely to slip and fall to the ground while learning to climb.

Protecting poultry and game

Most complaints about pine martens relate to them killing chickens or stealing their eggs before their human owners can collect them. Similarly, a pen full of pheasant poults is awfully tempting for a hungry pine marten, and they can cause havoc to the gamekeeper's precious charges after climbing up and over the wire mesh walls, followed by consternation when only one of the many slaughtered birds is removed. Elsewhere in Europe pine martens predate other domestic birds and their eggs. In the Netherlands, for example, Henri Wijsman of the WBN has several records of pine martens entering dovecotes to kill valuable doves and pigeons and to steal their eggs: in 2007, in the Heerde District one pine marten killed

37 pigeons (valued at 200 Euros each) in one night and stored them all in a tiny loft space where it was later discovered fast asleep on top of its feathery hoard. In all cases the losses are infuriating, but there are sustainable ways of avoiding them through simple good husbandry.

One simple solution for protecting poultry against a mainly nocturnal predator like the pine marten – which is already catching on in the Scottish Highlands – is to install a cunning battery-operated device that responds to changing light levels to open and shut the hen-house door at dawn and dusk respectively. It is available from a British firm for less than £100 and, although the aluminium sheet door looks disturbingly like a guillotine, it actually opens and closes very slowly so the hens don't take fright and have time to decide which side of the door they want to be. This means that poultry-keepers don't need to dash home at dusk to shut their birds in because the job is done automatically.

Pine martens are slim, agile climbers, so they are more difficult to exclude from game and poultry pens, dovecotes and hen houses than are most other predators; any standard pen without a wire mesh roof will not keep martens out because they can easily climb up and over the wire walls, or even jump from overhanging tree branches. A desperate adult marten, especially the more lightly built female, can reportedly squeeze through a gap as narrow as 45 millimetres, so any pen, dovecote or hen house that is not secure and well-maintained may allow access to hungry local martens. Trapping and removing martens is illegal without a licence, and licencing authorities are unlikely to grant a licence – especially if husbandry is not top-notch – because another marten will soon move in to occupy the territory left vacant by any animal removed; so, we need lasting solutions that don't involve eradicating pine martens (again). We also need people within the poultry-keeping and game shooting communities who have the vision, wit and courage to show their fellows the way forward.

Kevin Sadler of the Kilcormac Gun Club in Offaly is my Irish hero. In response to the recent recovery of pine martens in his county, which led to losses of pheasant poults on local shoots, he has taken the lead in designing marten-proof pheasant release pens. With advice from the VWT's Kate McAney, Kevin has made simple additions and amendments to the basic pheasant pen design that effectively exclude pine martens and other predators: a new waist-high electric mesh fence is installed outside the existing release pen as a first line of defence; then further electric wires are fitted around the top of the release pen to deter any pine marten that gets past the first fence and tries to climb into the pen; 40-centimetre-high galvanised metal sheeting is dug into the ground against the outside mesh of the pen to prevent digging and to act as a visual barrier between predators and prey; a soft mesh netting 'roof' is fitted over the pen (mainly to exclude buzzards); and finally any overhanging tree branches are trimmed back so as to remove opportunities for the local marten to make an aerial invasion. These tweaks cost 150 Euros per 50 metres of pen perimeter, amounting to about 1,000 Euros for a typical release pen, which Kevin believes is affordable to shoots in his area.

Having demonstrated that pheasant poult losses can be reduced to zero with nothing more harmful to the local pine martens than a mild electric shock, Kevin is now promoting these simple measures among neighbouring gun clubs. He has also shown the wider game shooting community that there is a modern, intelligent way to respond to predation problems. If only there were more like him!

In the 1990s, Liz Balharry did similar work with shooting estates and poultry-keepers in the Scottish Highlands: she showed that external electric wires were effective at preventing pine marten invasions; and a floppy electrified wire mesh overhang fitted to pheasant release pens was an additional defence against an especially determined marten. She showed me a video in which a local marten was effectively 'trained' to stay away from a pheasant release pen after receiving an electric shock – a legal and sustainable alternative to un-licenced marten killing or removal, in which case a new and naïve marten will soon arrive to try its luck. Despite Liz and the VWT promoting these simple measures at game fairs, country shows and via leaflets, there is little evidence they have been adopted on shooting estates in Scotland. So, I wonder how are they are protecting their penned game?

Sustainable egg-collection?
Although most reported encounters between pine martens and poultry involve predation of the birds themselves (where poor husbandry allows a marten to gain access), there are recent and reliable reports from Scotland, Holland and France of martens entering hen houses at night to

remove eggs without harming a single hen. I first heard about this non-lethal egg-harvesting behaviour from Matt Wilson who, through a hole he had constructed in the wood panelling, watched a pine marten visit a hen house at night to remove fresh-laid eggs from beneath a sitting hen on Morvern in the West of Scotland; he clearly saw the predator gently push its muzzle under the hen in order to grip each egg. In the same area Matt knows of two other people who had been losing eggs to martens at night without a single hen killed.

This non-lethal egg-collecting behaviour is apparently not unique: among many instances of chicken-killing by pine martens in the Netherlands, my Dutch friends have photographic evidence of a wild adult pine marten visiting a crowded hen-house at night from which it removed eggs and did not kill any of the bantams that laid them; the same animal (recognisable because part of its tail was missing) later visited another pen 1.5 kilometres away, where again it removed eggs but did not harm the bantams. In the Veluwe area, a different pine marten frequently entered a pen to take the eggs of bantams and guinea fowl, but did not harm the birds themselves. And in France a stone marten was filmed removing hens' eggs without causing any harm as it passed close to the roosting birds inside the hen-house.

This non-lethal harvesting of poultry products by pine martens may be unusual, though it could be more common than it appears simply because it is much less likely to be detected than is the predation of adult birds. Nevertheless, I cannot help but view the restraint involved as a sign of unusual intelligence in a carnivore that is fully capable of killing all the hens or bantams in a hen-house. If only we knew what thought-processes are involved as a marten enters a hen-house and makes the decision to select an egg instead of the more substantial and nutritious hen sitting upon it! It is tempting to regard it as a significant step along the evolutionary road towards coexistence between a cheeky carnivore and its human providers.

Illegal trapping and killing of pine martens
Illegal killing or removal of pine martens continues in areas where the species is perceived by certain interests as undesirable and where there is no interest in developing new and sustainable solutions to conflicts.

Whilst offences by gamekeepers against birds of prey receive most publicity and legal action, we can be sure that similarly dark deeds are affecting protected carnivores like the pine marten. I know this through conversations with trusted contacts who work alongside the people who freely admit to deliberately killing pine martens, mostly on shooting estates with a focus on producing large numbers of pheasants or grouse, but also in areas where martens kill poultry and cause other nuisances.

There are two main reasons why illegal killing of pine martens is much less likely to come to light than similar offences against birds of prey: firstly, even where pine martens are common, they are seen much less often than, say, buzzards, hen harriers or peregrines, so their disappearance is less likely to be noticed; and secondly, there are no mammal organisations equivalent to the RSPB and Raptor Study Groups, with vigilant staff and/or members who invest time and effort in detecting and reporting evidence of illegal persecution of birds of prey; so for both these reasons people can do illegal things to pine martens with greater confidence that they will evade detection – especially if those acts take place in remote areas.

This problem is most severe on those shooting estates with ruthless attitudes towards the removal of predators, such as in north-east Scotland (similar attitudes may be hindering the recovery of martens elsewhere in Scotland, including their spread south into England). Evidence from national pine marten distribution surveys suggests that, towards the end of the twentieth century, illegal killing of pine martens delayed the species' recolonisation of this area relative to other parts of Scotland into which pine martens spread back more quickly because of the lower levels of predator control. Subsequently, despite a wide-scale recovery, continued removal of pine martens on some estates means that in some areas populations are locally reduced and the species has a patchy distribution at best. Further west, where traditional estates have less emphasis on intensive shooting of gamebirds, there are signs of a softening of attitudes and there is now rather less illegal killing of pine martens. For example, on one western Scottish peninsula an average of 60 pine martens was killed illegally each winter in the mid-1980s and this has now declined to 12 or less, with a focus now on removing only the most troublesome animals. But attitudes are very slow to change and there is still much work to do.

Part of the problem lies in the non-specific nature of the lethal spring traps designed and used to kill so-called 'small ground vermin' species such as stoats, weasels, mink, rats and grey squirrels. By law these traps must be set in tunnels (hence the alternative name of 'tunnel traps') and practitioners are obliged to restrict the size of the tunnel entrance so as to avoid injury to protected species such as polecats and pine martens. Despite the development of an effective exclusion device by the GWCT, in my experience many tunnel traps do not exclude animals the size of a pine marten, so they are very much at risk if they stray on to those shooting estates where high densities of tunnel traps are deployed.

One might have thought that positive change would lie in the Agreement on International Humane Trapping Standards (AIHTS), a European Union initiative launched in 2008 to improve standards of humaneness in wildlife trapping. However, because the agreement relates only to trapping of certain mammals for their fur, and because the stoat is the only UK/Irish species listed that may be trapped without a licence, the scope for change is rather limited. Currently the most widely used traps for killing stoats – lethal spring traps that should be set in tunnels with restricted entrances so as to avoid harm to non-target species – do not comply with AIHTS because they take too long to kill the animals. The deadline for compliance with the AIHTS passed in July 2016, but the UK Government has apparently negotiated a two-year extension to allow more time for compliant stoat traps to be developed and tested. If these new 'faster-kill' traps are set in future in tunnels that allow entry by larger species, then nothing will have changed and non-target protected mammals such as pine martens will continue to be injured or killed. Furthermore, the non-compliant spring traps may continue to be used if trappers argue that they are not using them to target stoats but other non-protected mammals such as mink, grey squirrels, rats or weasels.

Moving pine martens
In both Ireland and Scotland, an increasingly common response among people who cannot tolerate pine martens is to live-trap and relocate them as an alternative to killing them, though this non-lethal approach is also illegal without a licence and it doesn't truly solve the problem because another marten is very likely to replace the one removed. Pine martens are

easy to catch in live-traps and, once trapped, they appear surprisingly calm (although a wild marten in a cage trap in close proximity to a human is probably highly stressed); so, transporting a live one in a cage trap in the back of a car is not necessarily an unpleasant experience for the driver. By this means many 'nuisance' pine martens are released some distance from their capture sites (and many probably make their way back home again).

Feeding and watching pine martens

As wide-ranging foragers with a passion for readily available treats like peanuts, raisins, honey, jam and eggs, pine martens can easily be tempted to visit feeding stations to provide wonderful viewing opportunities; and now that they have less reason to fear humans than 100 years ago those feeding stations can be very close to, or even inside, our dwellings. I am typing this section in late July in a holiday cottage on Ardnamurchan in the west of Scotland, with a pine marten feeding station on a round stone 'table' three metres away outside the window. Most days we have enjoyed fine close views of pine martens, often in broad daylight, feasting on peanuts scattered on the table. Emma (from whom we have rented the feeding station, with cottage attached) tells us that she has three different martens visiting currently, as well as a badger that tends to come later at night. Emma's mother, who lives nearby in the same village, has a visiting pine marten named 'Mrs P' that has got to know her so well that it takes food from her hand.

I first heard about pine martens enjoying human food in the 1980s, when there were stories of Scottish foresters sharing their jam butties with them. People's habit of feeding and watching pine martens at their houses is now very widespread across the Scottish Highlands; it is less common in Ireland, but knowing some of my soft-hearted Irish friends they won't be far behind. It grew from the martens' habit, as persecution declined and they dared to frequent the vicinity of human habitations again in the hope of an easy meal, of visiting bird feeders to eat peanuts until, with their arguably greater appeal, martens became the main focus or, as in Emma's case, feeding stations became dual-purpose with a seed-based day shift for the birds and a peanut, raisin, honey and jam evening shift for the pine martens. An internet search shows just how many Scottish holiday lets promote the possibility of pine marten viewing if you put out the right food; and similarly there are wildlife hides available to rent for watching and photographing pine martens. With many years of collective experience these businesses have developed some simple methods that increase our chances of a successful encounter with a wild pine marten; here are a few tips that work well at a feeding station outside the window of a living room or hide:

- Get the martens accustomed to having an outside electric light on from dusk onwards, so that the feeding station is illuminated after dark (and it's best if you turn the lights off inside so the martens cannot see you moving about);
- Avoid excessive, sudden noises inside the dwelling or hide that might alarm the martens and delay their visit to the feeding station;
- If you want to exclude foxes and badgers from the feeding station, make sure it is on an elevated platform above ground so that only pine martens can climb up to it;
- Provide food that is small and 'bitty', rather than big and chunky, so that a marten decides to stay on the feeding station to eat it rather than carry it off to eat out of sight; whole peanuts or smears of peanut butter are perfect in this respect and relatively healthy;
- Put the food out at about the same time relative to dusk each evening, so that the local pine martens get to know when it is worth visiting;

putting food out around dusk also helps to prevent too much of it being consumed by the day shift, such as birds and squirrels;
- Avoid foods that are high in processed sugars and fat, as these may compromise the health of the local pine martens;
- Keep pets away from the feeding station, especially dogs that might leave scent to strike fear into marten hearts and prevent them from visiting;
- Look for differences in the appearance and behaviour of any martens that you see, as this may help you to determine how many individuals are visiting the feeding station; some animals may be distinguished on the basis of body size and/or throat patterns and whether they are confident or nervous; also, look for the presence of testes and teats, which are usually visible in adult martens in summer but not in juveniles;
- And if it's late and you can stay awake no longer, set up a camera trap to record marten visits to the feeding station while you sleep!

It is fair to ask what impacts these feeding stations might have on the health, behaviour and survival of pine martens. Just as with feeding birds, any impacts, whether positive or negative, are probably linked to the quantity and quality of food available, as well as the time of year that it is provided. I believe that good food provided in summer helps hard-pressed breeding females to remain in good bodily condition while rearing their kits, as well as being a nutritional stop-gap for young martens as they start to become independent; it may also provide a boost for adult males during the late summer mating season, enabling them to invest more time and energy in searching for receptive females and creating next year's marten kits. So, there are likely to be various benefits to pine marten survival arising from summer feeding. But what about the disbenefits?

Some people worry that provision of abundant food by humans may prevent pine martens from hunting for themselves, and that they may become over-dependent upon feeding stations, with serious consequences if ever feeding ceases for any reason. I don't share these concerns because each pine marten is driven by a powerful urge to maintain and exploit a territory large enough to sustain it in the long-term. In the absence of human food provision that territory may provide occasional feasts, such as a fresh deer carcass, but that doesn't prevent the resident marten from foraging over the remainder of its patch. At Emma's feeding station the martens don't come every night, and when they do the visits are typically brief, suggesting that they spend most of their time busy elsewhere in their territories. So, just as with birds, feeding stations may boost pine marten survival without significantly influencing behaviour, possibly.

One likely consequence of attracting pine martens to feeding stations is an increase in the frequency of close-quarters interactions between individual martens keen to share the food provided. There must also be more interactions between martens and other carnivores attracted to feeding stations, such as foxes and badgers (I watched two pine martens feeding within a metre of a badger at the same feeding station outside our holiday cottage on Ardnamurchan). Many feeding stations in Scotland are visited by at least three pine martens, with some people reporting up to six or seven in late summer when semi-independent kits are present.

Observers report differences in the demeanour of martens at feeding stations, with some individuals appearing confident and relaxed while others seem nervous and wary when they visit. This may simply reflect differences in personality or, more likely, the contrast between resident territory-holders and intruders keen to avoid the resident; such differences are likely to be reinforced by aggression from residents towards intruders, which might occasionally involve physical attacks. I have received reports of several pine martens with facial injuries – consistent with bites made by other martens – visiting feeding stations in the west of Scotland, although there is no evidence that this was a direct consequence of aggression at feeding stations.

There is one serious risk associated with tempting pine martens to come close to houses for food, and that lies in the fact that not everyone likes pine martens and some people are willing to break the law to do them harm. Of course, a pine marten cannot initially tell the difference between a 'friendly' house and a 'dangerous' one, so it is unwise to establish a feeding station if another property nearby is occupied by someone likely to harm any martens that visit.

Holiday cottages with a 'marten option' and other wildlife-viewing businesses have become an important part of the rural economy where pine martens are common, facilitating sustainable eco-tourism by 'training' their local pine martens to perform for those of us who are happy to travel from marten-free places and pay good money for the chance of a close encounter with one of our most attractive wild mammals. The RSPB estimates that the reintroduced sea eagles on Mull have recently boosted the local tourism economy by some £5 million per year; and the Galloway Red Kite Trail has contributed tourism revenue of £8 million per year in the region. I believe that pine martens across Scotland have had a similarly beneficial effect. There are encouraging signs that recognition of these commercial benefits has led to increased tolerance of pine martens on some traditional sporting estates in the Scottish Highlands.

An evening with Pat and James's martens

Retired couple Pat and James Hislop belong to that growing band of Scots who feel very fortunate to share their lives with pine martens. They live in a modern house surrounded by woodland on the Black Isle near Inverness, and pine martens visit their veranda most evenings to enjoy the food set out for them. Pat and James are extra special because they are so keen to share 'their' pine martens with other enthusiasts. Many people, including me in September 2015, have enjoyed their generous hospitality while watching a delightful marten show, with a well-informed running commentary from our hosts about who is who and what their feeding preferences are. The evening starts with a careful laying out of the feast on the veranda and just inside the living room: rows of individual jam tarts and fruit pies; custard cream biscuits and chocolate bars; fresh dead day-old chicks and hens eggs; and little bowls of sweet honey water to wash it all down.

Before the first four-legged guests arrived, I was introduced to some of them in James's book of photographs and in videos recorded on his camera traps. Differences in body size, behaviour and throat patterns enable Pat and James to recognise their regulars instantly, and to spot any new martens not seen before. The most frequent visitors tend to be adult female martens with, in summer, their dependent kits. In summer 2015, Pat and James identified at least seven martens: it was the adult females Sandra, Nadia and their four kits (two each) that spent most time enjoying Pat and James's hospitality; and there were less frequent visits by a large adult male called 'Lefty', who sometimes tried to mate with the adult females after sharing the feast with them.

Pat and James say that June and July are the best times to watch martens because hard-pressed mothers and their dependent kits visit nightly to take advantage of the extra food provided, and dusk falls late around the longest day. When I joined them in September the marten families had broken up, so there were fewer diners at the restaurant and darkness fell much earlier. Nevertheless, it was thrilling when the first marten – a slim female still in her dark, sleek summer coat – loped across the dusky lawn, jumped effortlessly on to the veranda and headed straight for the custard creams. While Pat and James were debating whether it was Sandra or Nadia, a bigger marten moved in beside her to sample the goods. This male – was it Lefty? – seemed hungry and fearless as he stepped noiselessly through the open French windows to explore the treats laid out on the living room floor. With just the briefest glance at the open-mouthed man quivering on the sofa two metres away, he selected a fresh chick and carried it out on to the veranda and away.

This was a fairly average evening for Pat and James and, as I started breathing again and brought my heart rate down, they kindly shared memories of other martens they had got to know over the years. Their observations revealed subtle individual differences in behaviour and demeanour, as well as some fascinating interactions between martens. Most heart-warming of all were the tales of confiding animals prepared to approach Pat on the sofa and put their forepaws up beside her to take treats from her hand. I was left with a blend of envy and admiration for my hosts: envy for how their lives are enriched so simply by their nightly encounters with an enchanting wild mammal; and admiration for the wonder and respect they accord the animals, and the gracious way in which they share their good fortune with others.

REINTRODUCTIONS AND TRANSLOCATIONS

Covert releases
Pine martens are not difficult to catch where they are common, so private translocations between marten strongholds and other areas have probably been happening for many years for different reasons. For example, in the 1980s some Irish wildlife rangers used to 'rescue' pine martens from areas where they were likely to be persecuted and relocate them to less populated areas where their chances of survival were higher.

Although now illegal without a small forest of licences and permissions, covert captures and translocations are apparently still undertaken by those prepared to ignore the law. Inevitably information on such releases rarely comes to light, and there is no proper monitoring to determine whether such projects succeed or fail and why.

The recent establishment of a new population of pine martens on the Scottish island of Mull is very likely a consequence of people – perhaps mischievously – moving pine martens from the mainland where they were deemed to be a nuisance. And genetic evidence gathered by the VWT suggests that some of the pine martens found in England and Wales around the turn of the millennium had come south from Scotland with human help: for example, there is at least one recent admission that about seven pine martens were released in the west of England between the 1980s and 2000s after their capture on a Scottish shooting estate (they were reportedly handed to an intermediary on the understanding that they would not be released in Scotland).

Apart from the illegality involved in the capture and covert relocation of pine martens, and the associated uncertainties relating to animal welfare, disease transmission and lack of monitoring, an infuriating consequence of such schemes is the way they cloud our understanding of natural patterns of population establishment and expansion. Worst of all, they undermine the efforts of those who work hard to do things properly by following the correct procedures designed to ensure a successful translocation.

The VWT's Pine Marten Recovery Project

Among several exciting mammally things happening in Britain and Ireland in the early decades of the new millennium, this one has given me the greatest thrill. Meticulously planned and brilliantly executed, the VWT's efforts to reinforce the sparse populations of pine martens in southern Britain have set the Gold Standard for similar projects in future. After years of painstaking work to detect the presence of pine martens struggling to survive in their historical strongholds in Wales and England, in which I confess to having played a part, the genetic evidence collated by Neil Jordan of the VWT led us to the conclusion that the relict, post-decline populations of haplotype *i* pine martens had probably fizzled out and been replaced by animals covertly translocated from Scotland and by escapes from captivity.

This new genetic evidence meant that one area of concern – that restocking with pine martens of the 'wrong' haplotype might lead to the loss of precious genes lurking in the modern descendants of relict populations – had become less of a constraint upon recovery plans, although it still seemed premature to declare haplotype *i* extinct in southern Britain. So, in 2012, the VWT began beavering away at a cunning recovery plan designed to restore healthy populations of pine martens to England and Wales. The prudent first step was a lengthy bout of stakeholder consultation to ensure broad support for the general idea of restocking as the mechanism for pine marten recovery, followed by a detailed two-year feasibility study undertaken by the supremely unflappable Jenny Macpherson.

The VWT's feasibility study identified candidate sites in southern Britain where reinforcement of struggling marten populations was most likely to succeed, with the extensive forests hugging the flanks of the Cambrian Mountains in mid-Wales top of the list. Discussions with SNH and FES led to agreement on the removal of a small number of martens from each of several marten-rich forests across the Scottish Highlands, including field assessments before and after removal to ensure that there were no lasting ill-effects on populations (tellingly, a senior official of one of the Scottish organisations commented wryly that the translocated martens would be safer in Wales than in parts of Scotland where illegal persecution is still rife).

The initial plan was to move a total of 40 Scottish martens over two years

(2015 and 2016). Meanwhile, back down in Wales, David Bavin continued explaining the project and building relationships with local communities and landowners in and around the chosen release area (wisely the VWT had decided to limit publicity so that local people would hear about the project from themselves first-hand rather than through the national media). Other work in the release area included assessments of prey populations to ensure that the Scottish martens would find plenty to eat.

Because the project would involve the capture, transport and release of protected wild animals between and through three different countries (Scotland, England and Wales), including sedation, veterinary health screening and the fitting of radio collars, it required a staggering array of licences and consents from several organisations not all famed for their speed of response. Fortunately, Jenny and her team had started the application process a year in advance, so had time to wrestle calmly with a number of unexpected requests and conditions that might otherwise have delayed the project and destroyed their sanity. Thankfully, they were ready to start with the first bout of live-trapping in autumn 2015, and I was privileged to be up there in the Scottish Highlands to help. The trapping was very successful and, after careful veterinary assessment, twenty adult martens were selected, fitted with radio collars and driven in batches down to the release site in mid-Wales.

The translocated Scottish martens were 'soft released' in stages from large cages supplied by Chester Zoo, in which fresh food and resting sites remained available in case the martens needed a bit of support post-release. With the exception of one greedy female – nicknamed 'Miss Piggy' – which kept revisiting the release pens to gobble up the food provided, the newly arrived martens ranged widely and tested the radio-tracking skills of the VWT's David Bavin and Josie Bridges and their volunteer assistants. By mid-November 2015, there were 20 Scottish martens exploring the forested slopes of the Cambrian Mountains due east of Aberystwyth. It was fascinating to plot their movements with the VWT radio-tracking team as each marten gradually settled into a stable home range and started leaving scats on forest tracks to advertise their occupancy.

This phase of the project was not without its challenges and pitfalls. The martens were not all easy to follow across the rugged terrain of mid-

Wales, and contact was lost with one or two for weeks at a time when they temporarily vacated the release area for their own reasons. There were some fatalities in the first winter, which was exceptionally wet and windy. But most of the radio-tagged animals stayed put and, in summer 2016, there came the exciting news that at least four litters of marten kits had been born to radio-tagged females in the 'new' Welsh population. This was the icing on the cake that we hoped for, and gave us every reason to be optimistic that the population would establish and expand. Further autumn translocations of 19 Scottish pine martens in 2016 and 12 in 2017 brought to 51 the total number released into mid-Wales.

Following the successful start to the VWT's reinforcement project, a new project led by Gloucestershire Wildlife Trust has started, with the first releases in 2019, to establish a pine marten population in the Forest of Dean, close to the border between England and Wales.

STUDYING PINE MARTENS

There are many ways of learning about pine martens, some of which are expensive, hi-tech and/or involve the need for special research licences, such as radio-tracking, genetic analysis and the removal of whiskers to derive dietary information via stable isotope analysis. Since these methods tend to be out of reach of those of us not attached to a university or research institution, I have concentrated on the more accessible and affordable ones below.

I have already written about the value of scats in studies of pine martens, and it is fair to point out that this faecal obsession is a rather British/Irish affair. Elsewhere in the pine marten's range other approaches are in vogue, with the Scandinavians relying on winter snow to find and follow footprints to study marten behaviour, and the Dutch focus on searching for and monitoring tree holes occupied by their martens, especially during the breeding season. Nevertheless, thanks to our pine martens' habit of pooing on the very woodland tracks we walk along, there is much to learn about them once you have got your eye (and nose) in.

The new kid on the block, of course, is camera trapping, which has enabled people to learn about their local pine martens. Camera traps are discreet, battery-powered units that are triggered by the movement or heat of an animal's body. At night, they use infra-red light to illuminate their targets and can be programmed to record digital images or short videos. They work best where the camera is aimed at a source of food that is attractive to pine martens, such as peanuts in a tree-mounted feeder, or a mixture of peanuts, honey and raisins spread on the ground (although bait on the ground carries the risk of non-target species like badgers and foxes filling the memory card with their images, so it is always best to place bait in an elevated location requiring good climbing skills).

Since clear photographic images are generally more reliable than field signs such as footprints and scats (unless DNA analysis is involved with the latter), camera traps have led to an increase in high quality records of pine martens to inform distribution maps of the species. For example, in north-east Scotland, about half of the recent pine marten records for a new mammal atlas (published early in 2017) came from camera traps. In Northern Ireland, David Tosh led a very successful citizen science project in 2015 in which camera traps trained on peanut feeders were deployed at 348 sites in 137 hectads; seventy volunteers were involved in checking the cameras and replenishing the bait and thanks to their efforts images of pine martens were recorded in 79 per cent of hectads covered.

Another use of camera traps has been to capture images of the bib pattern of pine martens as a means to identify different individuals – very useful where biologists need to know how many martens live in a particular area. In order to maximise the success of this approach in his study of pine martens in the Netherlands, Erwin van Maanen developed the 'jiggler' – based on a steel clamshell tea infuser – containing a smelly treat mounted on the end of a stiff but springy wire some 1.2 metres long. The effect of this device was to encourage the pine martens to rear up and pose in front of the camera trap in a position that best recorded images of their individually variable bib patterns.

Because camera traps allow us to record video footage at any time of the day or night, their value to pine marten researchers is immense: they allow us to watch intriguing patterns of behaviour, like the pine marten's 'hip-wiggle', as well as social interactions between individuals; and they have revealed how pine martens interact with other species attracted to feeding stations, such as foxes, badgers and squirrels. As part of his PhD research the VWT's David Bavin is using camera traps to understand how differences in the character of individual radio-tagged pine martens – with some being noticeably bolder than others – influence their ranging and territorial behaviour in the wild.

Some people have successfully installed miniature video cameras inside den boxes occupied by pine martens, with a live link to a screen inside their houses. Most famously, in 2016 and 2017, a couple in the West of Scotland made regular video posts on Facebook under the title *Pine Marten Diaries*, which revealed some wonderful behaviour, including charming footage of a mother and her two young kits. However, two caveats are appropriate: firstly, in Galloway Forest the publicity-shy pine martens took exception to the video cameras installed inside the den boxes by Forestry Commission Scotland and destroyed the wiring so that none of the units worked for very long; and secondly, it is important to ensure that any camera-related fiddling at a pine marten den box does not involve breaking the law that protects the animal from disturbance at its resting site.

PINE MARTENS AND THE LAW

The pine marten currently receives thorough legal protection in both Britain and Ireland, with separate pieces of legislation delivering a similar level of cover in different parts of these islands. This convergence arises because our wildlife laws have common origins in international legal instruments like the Bern Convention and the European Union's Habitats Directive (under which the pine marten is listed on Appendix III and Annexe V respectively). As an example, since 1988 in Scotland it has been illegal recklessly or deliberately to kill, injure or take a pine marten; and a licence is required from Scottish Natural Heritage to trap a pine marten in any situation. It is also illegal to damage, destroy or obstruct access to a pine marten den site, except when this is within a dwelling house; and, unless it is a non-breeding adult in a dwelling house, it is illegal to disturb a pine marten at its den site without an appropriate licence. However, you should not rely on the above interpretation if you require detailed advice on the pine marten's legal protection; instead please approach the relevant country agency (see *Sources of information*, page 190).

In some parts of their large Eurasian range, pine martens may be 'harvested' as game animals or killed as pests without the need for a licence. In Russia, for example, pine martens are trapped for their fur in many areas, where efforts to avoid over-hunting involve quotas that limit the removal of more than 35 per cent of the number of martens estimated to be present. Clearly one can only have confidence in this approach as a means to maintain healthy populations if the methods of estimating numbers are scientifically sound and reliable.

Closer to home, pine martens may be killed in some countries in Western Europe where EU-wide Directives require member states to maintain populations at 'favourable conservation status'. In France, for example, since a Government Order in 1987 the pine marten has been listed as a game species that may be hunted during the correct season; and in 1988 it was added to the list of pest species, along with other mustelids such as the weasel and polecat, that may be killed throughout the year. The hunting of game animals and the destruction of pests are viewed as separate activities – involving different methods – hence the separate lists; but it is not unusual for some species, like the pine marten, to occur on both lists.

According to French government figures, in a typical year since 2011 the pine marten was classed as a pest in 22 out of 96 départements (the stone marten was so classed in 70 départements); 5,483 pine martens were killed per year as pests (compared with 18,041 stone martens); and 8,871 pine martens (and 17,762 stone martens) were killed across France as game animals per year. So, across the great majority of départements, pine martens are not classed as pests (but stone martens are); nevertheless, in a typical year, combined pest/game totals of more than 14,000 pine martens and approaching 36,000 stone martens are currently killed in France.

PINE MARTENS AND COMMERCIAL FORESTRY

Modern forestry can have substantial impacts upon pine martens, especially where huge clear fells remove areas of foraging and resting habitat in a matter of days, converting blocks of high forest to open ground that remains unattractive to pine martens for ten years or more; and where conifer crops are harvested on a short rotation, for example to supply the pulpwood industry, forests become dominated by stands of young trees that represent permanently poor habitat for pine martens. We can expect that this scale and intensity of management will adversely affect the viability of individual home ranges and, thereby, the stability and density of marten populations.

In his study of Irish pine martens' spatial use of a commercial conifer forest in County Leitrim, Declan O'Mahony found that pine martens were apparently absent in large parts of his study area subject to recent harvesting. He suggested that perhaps martens chose not to establish home ranges in areas of forest subject to disturbance and habitat fragmentation related to harvesting, with the possible additional influence of a physiological stress response where individuals are seriously disturbed by clear-felling, for example. This must limit the capacity of commercial forests to support the same number of pine martens as those found in undisturbed forests. Indeed, in forests in eastern Europe, Vadim Sidorovich has reported that intensive felling rates limited the population density of pine martens there.

Nevertheless, on balance, modern forestry, especially when managed according to certification schemes like the UK Woodland Assurance Standard and in compliance with the UK Forestry Standards, is an overwhelmingly positive force in the conservation of pine marten populations on our largely deforested islands. This is because the UK's and Ireland's forestry policies have encouraged increasing areas of woodland cover without which marten populations cannot thrive. Above all, there is great strategic significance for pine marten conservation in those conifer forests established in the twentieth century that are now owned and managed by the various government agencies in Britain and

Ireland. Although many are located on poor, upland soils (where land was cheap so huge areas could be purchased and planted), these forests are vital refuges for pine martens because they tend to be large (so they are structurally diverse and harvesting events affect only a small proportion of the area), predator control is limited or absent (so there is a low risk of an early, violent death for pine martens), there are low human population densities (so few opportunities for conflicts with pine martens) and the ownership is sympathetic and accountable.

So, despite the adverse impacts of major harvesting events and their aftermaths, forestry is ultimately the saviour and friend of the pine marten; and environmentally minded foresters are working to minimise the impacts of their activities. Similarly, FES has been conducting its own ongoing research to improve detection and protection of sensitive pine marten sites – such as occupied natal dens – subject to forestry operations, with buffer zones and timing constraints playing a key part.

The constraints arising from the scarcity of sheltered, elevated pine marten den sites in commercial forests have been explored above. Although tree-mounted den boxes are a viable option, forestry bodies could make a huge contribution by incorporating snug pine marten den spaces in the roofs of their buildings. From toilet blocks to visitor centres (think of the educational video-viewing!), from workshops to deer larders and mountain bike stores, there are myriad opportunities to provide safe roof-level marten dens away from timber harvesting activities.

FURTHER READING

The Vincent Wildlife Trust has also produced good leaflets, usually in collaboration with other relevant organisations, which offer advice to people on how to conserve and coexist with pine martens.

The following VWT leaflets can be downloaded free from www.vwt.org.uk/downloads

Managing forest and woodlands for pine martens
(produced with the forestry consultancy SelectFor)

The Pine Marten in Ireland – a guide for householders
(produced with the Irish National Parks and Wildlife Service)

How to exclude pine martens from game and poultry pens
(produced with the Irish National Parks and Wildlife Service)

Constructing, erecting and monitoring Pine Marten Den Boxes
(produced with the Irish Environmental Network)

Living with Pine Martens – a guide to the pine marten in Scotland
(produced with Scottish Natural Heritage)

SOURCES OF INFORMATION AND ADVICE

The Mammal Society: www.mammal.org.uk

The Vincent Wildlife Trust: www.vwt.org.uk

National Parks and Wildlife Service (Republic of Ireland): www.npws.ie

Department of Agriculture, Environment and Rural Affairs (Northern Ireland): www.daera-ni.gov.uk/articles/wildlife-licensing

Scottish Natural Heritage: www.snh.gov.uk

Natural Resources Wales: www.naturalresources.wales

Natural England: www.gov.uk/government/organisations/natural-england

The Martes Working Group: www.eko.uj.edu.pl/mwg/

INDEX

abdominal gland 116, 118–19, 130
activity levels/patterns/timing 38, 73, 95–6, 104, 145, 147, 149, 153
albinism 48
Aleutian disease 142
American marten 11–14, 28–9, 38, 51, 61, 119, 138
amphibians 37, 85, 102, 104–5, 108, 110
anal scent glands 27, 87, 117–18
Anthropocene 4
arboreal (including adaptations) 8, 15, 36–7, 40–4, 52, 69, 102, 108, 128, 146
Ardennes, France 38
Ariundle National Nature Reserve, Argyll 86
auto-marter/auto-marder 22–4

Back from the Brink (pine marten project) 66
baculum 21, 26, 130
badger 15, 36, 44, 55, 118, 120, 139, 145, 172, 175, 182–3
bank vole 103, 108–13, 144
basal metabolic rate 38
bats 71–2, 75, 78, 105–6, 139, 163–4
beech/stone marten 8–9, 16, 18, 20–1, 25, 32–5, 50
Beinn Eighe National Nature Reserve 88
Białowieża Forest 1, 38–9, 49, 73–5, 103–7, 109, 147–8
bib (extent, colour, patterning, variation) 20–1, 46–8, 66, 183
birds (in pine marten diet) 82, 85, 102, 104–5, 107–8, 110–11, 113–15, 127, 145, 166, 168
bird boxes (protection of/as den sites/food caches) 77, 115, 162–3
birds of prey 54, 67–8, 170
Black Isle, Scotland 90, 120, 160, 176
black stork (nest predation of) 102
black woodpecker 75–6, 78
body size/shape 15, 33, 36–44, 129, 147, 174, 176

breeding 4, 16, 22, 27, 55, 65, 67, 74–9, 87, 106, 119, 122–31, 136, 140, 149, 159, 161, 164–5, 174, 182
Bresse Region, France 130–1, 148–9
Burren 58, 159

caching of food 38, 114–15, 136
Cambrian Mountains 65, 179–80
camera-trapping 28, 47,66, 70, 73, 86, 93, 102, 117, 119, 123–4, 138, 145–6, 161, 174, 176, 182–4
capercaillie 150–4, 158
Carmarthenshire 7, 60–1, 63, 69
carrion 104, 108, 110, 114
Cheviot Hills, Northumberland 61
climate change 15, 149–51, 153–4
climbing 16, 20, 22, 37, 40–4, 48, 52, 58, 72, 74, 76, 79, 95, 102, 104, 128, 159, 162–3, 166–8, 173, 182
coexistence
    pine marten with stone marten 20, 146–9
    pine marten with humans 169, 189
collective noun (for pine martens) 9
communication 48, 80, 83, 88, 90, 116–21
competition 39, 73, 103, 105, 144, 147–9
cortisol 116
covert releases 63, 66, 178–9
crag mart 8, 34
Crom Estate, Fermanagh 86

defence 15, 27, 74, 90, 116, 168
delayed implantation 16, 104, 124
Department of Agriculture, Environment and Rural Affairs (Northern Ireland) 190
dens 16, 20, 38, 50–1, 74–9, 88, 95–6, 121, 126–8, 140, 145–6, 149, 164, 188
den boxes 78–9, 100, 118, 124, 127–8, 135–6, 164, 183–4, 188
dentition 44–5

190

diet/dietary analysis 68, 72, 84, 99, 102–14, 141, 144–5, 147–8, 182
diseases 137, 138–9, 141–2, 178
dispersal (e.g. by juvenile martens) 65, 95, 100, 129–30, 145
distribution of pine marten
  Eurasian 17–18, 29–30, 32, 99, 149
  Ireland and Britain 3, 49, 57–8, 64–6, 170
  Surveys 58, 60–3, 65, 90, 92, 155, 170, 182
DNA 64, 69, 72, 92–4, 132, 135, 182
Dromore Wood, County Clare 86, 99, 112

edible dormouse 75, 146
egg-stealing 102, 161, 163, 166, 168–9
evolution 15–16, 93, 169

facial injuries 138, 175
family life 119–20, 127–31, 161, 164–6, 177
feeding pine martens 47–8, 101, 117, 119–20, 138, 172–7, 183
field signs 80–2
field vole 45, 68, 71, 110–11
fighting 138, 175
fisher 18–19
footprints 80–2, 160, 182
foraging 20, 38–9, 67, 70, 73, 96, 99, 102–4, 106, 108, 126–8, 148–9, 172, 174, 187
Forest Enterprise Scotland/FES 2, 78, 135–6, 152–3, 163, 179, 188
Forest of Dean, Gloucestershire 31, 181
Forestry Commission 60, 66, 134, 183
forestry (impacts upon pine martens) 59, 88, 154, 187–8
fossil record 15–16, 29, 32, 34, 49
foxes 20, 50–3, 55, 67–8, 71, 73–4, 87, 94, 103–4, 121–2, 137, 140, 144–6, 151, 153–4, 173, 175, 182–3
fox cubs (killed by pine marten) 145–6
fruit/frugivory 20, 22, 26–7, 85, 96, 99, 102,103, 105, 107–8, 110–14, 145, 148, 161–2, 176

fur/fur trade 9–10, 12–13, 16, 18, 20–1, 25–8, 33–4, 38, 42, 46–52, 56, 61, 80, 82, 85, 87, 126, 129, 139, 185

Galloway Forest 60, 65, 68, 78–9, 90, 92, 94, 124, 126–8, 132, 135–6, 183
Galloway Lite den box 79
Game and Wildlife Conservation Trust 151, 158, 171
game 4, 13, 33, 54, 56, 146, 150, 161, 166–8, 170, 185–6, 189
game shooting 13, 49, 54–5, 150, 167–8
gamekeepers 52, 54–9, 122, 158–9, 162, 166, 170
genetics 15–16, 18, 20, 27, 29, 30–2, 47–8, 61–3, 66, 93–4, 110, 133, 178–9, 182
genotype 30, 93
gestation 124, 130
glacial refuge 30–1, 33
Gorky Park 25
grey squirrel 114, 146, 154–7, 171
guard hairs 21, 46, 126

habitat
  fragmentation 67–8, 187
  loss 27, 55–6
  preference 8, 14, 29, 32, 50, 67, 70, 74, 102, 104, 109, 147–9
hair tube 133, 135
haplotype 30, 32, 47, 63, 179
hearing 37, 102
heraldry 10
hip-wiggle 84, 86–7, 117, 183
home range 39, 56, 67–8, 74, 80, 95–100, 129–30, 132, 180, 187
hunting (of pine martens with hounds) 34, 52–4, 56, 145
hybridisation 17, 20, 26, 61

illegal trapping/killing (of pine martens) 60, 167, 169–71, 178–9, 185
implantation (of blastocysts) 16, 95, 104, 124, 131
inter-canine distance (ICD) 82
invertebrates 75, 89, 102, 105, 107–8, 110, 112, 114, 145

IUCN listing 18–19, 27, 29

Japanese marten 17, 19, 28
jiggler 183

kidas 26
Kielder Forest, Northumberland 66
Killarney (including National Park) 52, 60, 112–13
Killavoggy, County Leitrim 98, 132–3
kits 39, 41, 59, 73–4, 76–8, 95–6, 116, 119–20, 122–30, 136–8, 140, 149, 157, 160–1, 164–6, 174, 176, 181, 183
Kuna 10

lactation 127, 157
Lakeland 34, 51, 53–4, 57, 61, 63, 66, 145
Landscape of fear 156
legal protection 55, 59, 62, 137, 150, 158–9, 164, 185
Leptospirosis 142
Leucistic 48
licence (for disturbance of pine martens) 78, 82, 151, 166–8, 171, 178, 180, 182, 185
lifespan 131
literature (references to pine martens) 12–13
litter size 122, 125–6
lynx 104, 137, 153–4

Mammal Society 14, 134, 138, 190
mating/mating season 26, 39, 74, 90, 95–6, 100, 116, 118–20, 122–4, 131, 174
Marderschutzanlage 24
martelism 100–1
Martes Complex 16–19
Martes vetus 16
Martes Working Group 11, 18, 22, 190
MARTRECS 62–3
media coverage 158–9, 180
mesopredator release 153
Microtus 109
mink 35, 39, 82, 102, 124, 139, 142, 159, 171

Morangie Forest 67–9, 71, 90, 98, 110–11
mortality 67, 122–3, 125, 137, 145
moult 34, 46–7, 95–6
Myotismart 90
mythology/mythical 10–11, 61

names (historical and foreign of pine marten) 6–9, 33
natal dens 41, 74–7, 95, 119, 122, 124, 126–9, 140, 164, 188
National Parks and Wildlife Service/ NPWS (Ireland) 158, 166, 189–90
Natural England 66, 190
Natural Resources Wales 190
Nietoperek 71–2
Nilgiri marten 18–19, 27–8
non-invasive methods 93, 132–6
Northumbria 63, 66
North Yorkshire Moors 63, 66
Novar Estate, Ross-shire 98, 132

oestrus 95, 120, 123
omnivory 84, 102, 108
otters 12, 15, 36, 44, 53, 55, 139

Pacific marten 19, 29, 41
parasites 128, 137–43
Pennines 57, 61, 66
persecution 31, 38, 49, 56, 59–60, 149, 164, 170, 173, 178–9
photographing pine martens 3, 14, 48, 63, 66, 70, 138, 146, 159, 173, 182
Pine Marten Diaries 1, 100, 127, 183
Pine Marten Recovery Project 31, 45, 65, 120, 130, 145, 179–81
Pine Marten Population Assessment (Ireland) 133–4
place names 7
play 164–5
poems (about pine martens) 12
polecat 4, 6, 15, 39, 45, 50, 55, 73, 82, 99, 122, 124, 139, 142, 171, 185
Polish Academy of Sciences 39, 75, 105–6, 147–8
population 4, 18–19, 27–30, 32, 47, 54–5, 57–65, 71, 79–80, 88, 93–4, 103–4, 109, 112, 122, 130–8, 143,

145, 147, 153–7, 162–3, 170, 178–81
  decline 49, 55–7, 62–3, 150
  density 68, 104, 132–6
  estimates 94, 132–6
  recovery 4, 25, 59–60, 63, 66, 122, 145, 155, 164, 178–81
poultry 4, 13, 33, 50, 161, 166–70, 189
Portlaw Woods, Waterford 90, 135–6, 138
predators (of pine martens) 32, 40, 67–71, 74, 95, 122, 128, 137, 144–5, 164
predator control/eradication 49–50, 55–6, 59–60, 62, 137, 170, 188
pregnancy 95, 122, 124

rabies 138–9
radio-tracking 57, 67–70, 73–4, 77, 97–8, 100, 105–6, 132–3, 137, 147, 180, 182
rat 113
red squirrel 110, 113, 140, 154–6
reinforcement/reintroduction 25, 60, 65, 138, 143, 150, 154, 176, 178–81
reptiles 105, 107–8, 110
resting/resting sites 20, 23, 37, 38, 67, 71, 74–9, 88, 95–6, 100, 102, 106, 109, 129, 140, 148, 164, 180, 184, 187
road casualties 40, 46, 69–70, 131, 137, 139, 142
rocky habitat/landscapes 7–8, 14, 53, 57–8, 60
rodents 10, 15, 20, 26, 37, 45, 68, 71, 85, 102–5, 109, 125–6, 142, 144–6
roof occupancy 20, 22, 77, 102, 130, 149, 159–61, 164–6, 188

sable 17–18, 20, 25–6, 51
Sarcoptic mange 140
scats
  abundance/density 89–91
  analysis (in diet studies) 72, 105, 110–14, 141
  deposition 76, 79, 82, 116–17, 180
  extraction of DNA from 69, 92–4, 132, 135–36
  scent 83–4, 159

size, colour and shape 84–7
  surveys 61–2, 64–5, 68, 88–91, 182
scat detection dogs 89, 91–3
scavenging 15, 26, 85, 105
scent glands 27, 87, 93, 116–19, 130
scent marking 93, 117–19, 123
Scottish Gamekeepers' Association 158
Scottish Highlands 4, 13–14, 33, 40, 57, 59, 60, 62, 66, 70, 90–1, 97, 118–19, 121, 122, 124, 130, 138, 142, 158, 162, 165, 167–8, 173, 176, 179, 180
Scottish Natural Heritage (SNH) 65, 78, 151, 166, 179, 185, 189–90
sexual dimorphism 38–9, 82, 105
Sheehy Effect 155–6
skeleton 34, 36–7, 42, 44, 142
Snowdonia 7, 57, 61, 63
snow-tracking 28, 51, 80, 82, 182
Speyside, NE Scotland 163
squirrel pox 154, 156
stoat 6, 15, 39, 46, 48, 55, 104, 122, 139, 141, 171
stone/beech marten 8–9, 16, 18, 20–1, 25, 32–5, 50
Strathspey 152
stress hormone 116–17
stress response 116, 120, 130, 166, 172, 187
sustainable conflict resolution 4, 152–3, 159, 161–8
Swift Ecology 1, 90

tail-swishing 120–1
tayra 18–19
Teagasc 134
'teenage' phase 100, 122, 130–1
territory/territoriality 24, 48, 73, 88, 90, 95, 97, 100, 105, 116, 119, 122–3, 135–6, 167, 174–5, 183
testosterone 118, 130
thermoregulation 25, 37–8, 41, 44, 104–5, 126, 164
ticks 139–40, 142
tooth wear 45, 131
translocation of pine martens to Wales 4, 31, 65, 110, 137, 145, 156, 178–81
trapping 51–2, 54–6, 91, 99, 133, 135, 167, 169, 171, 180

tree/arboreal cavities 16, 37, 67, 71, 74–6, 78, 106, 115, 126, 140, 164
tunnel or spring traps 51, 137, 171

underfur 20–1, 46
urine 93, 116–17, 127, 165

Vincent Wildlife Trust (VWT) 1, 31, 40, 45, 61–2, 65–6, 72–3, 76, 78–9, 86, 90–1, 94, 99, 110, 120, 130, 135, 137–8, 140, 143, 145, 156, 162, 166–8, 178–81, 183, 189–90
vocalisations 119–20, 123

Waabizheshi 11
watching pine martens 172–7
Waterford Institute of Technology 72, 92, 134

weaning 95, 125, 127, 129, 165
weasel 11, 15, 24, 39, 48–9, 51, 55, 99, 104, 122, 139, 141, 171, 185
Whitelee Forest, East Renfrewshire 92–3
wildcat 49, 70, 99
wildwood 4, 49, 56, 74, 103
Wildwood Trust, Kent 125
wolverine 11, 15, 18–19, 137
woodland clearance 49–50, 55–6
woodpecker holes/nest chambers 75–6, 78, 82, 128
Workgroep Boommarter Nederland 1, 76, 166

yellow-throated marten 17–19, 26–7
yellow-necked mouse 75, 103, 109